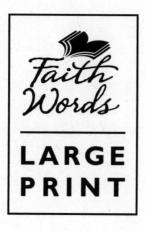

FaithWords

LARGE
PRINT

LET GOD FIGHT YOUR BATTLES

Being Peaceful in the Storm

JOYCE MEYER

LARGE PRINT

Unless otherwise indicated, all Scripture quotations are taken from the *Amplified Bible* (AMP). *The Amplified Bible*, Old Testament, copyright © 1965, 1987 by The Zondervan Corporation. *The Amplified New Testament*, copyright © 1954, 1958, 1987 by The Lockman Foundation. Used by permission.

Scripture quotations marked NIV are taken from the Holy Bible, New International Version®, NIV. Copyright © 1973, 1978, 1984 by International Bible Society. Used by permission of Zondervan Publishing House. All rights reserved.

Scripture quotations marked NKJV are taken from the New King James Version. Copyright © 1982 by Thomas Nelson, Inc. Used by permission. All rights reserved.

Scripture quotations marked KJV are taken from the King James Version of the Bible.

The author has emphasized some words in Scripture quotations. These words are not emphasized in the original Bible versions.

Scripture passages or verses paraphrased by the author are based on the *Amplified Bible* or the King James Version of the Bible.

Derived from material previously published in *The Battle Belongs to the Lord*.

FaithWords
Hachette Book Group
1290 Avenue of the Americas
New York, NY 10104

www.faithwords.com

Printed in the United States of America

RRD-C

First Edition: June 2015

10 9 8 7 6 5 4 3 2 1

FaithWords is a division of Hachette Book Group, Inc.
The FaithWords name and logo are trademarks of Hachette Book Group, Inc.

The Hachette Speakers Bureau provides a wide range of authors for speaking events. To find out more, go to www.hachettespeakersbureau.com or call (866) 376-6591.

The publisher is not responsible for websites (or their content) that are not owned by the publisher.

Library of Congress Cataloging-in-Publication Data

Meyer, Joyce, 1943–
    Let God fight your battles : begin peaceful in the storm / Joyce Meyer.—First [edition].
      pages cm
    ISBN 978-1-4555-8783-4 (hardcover) — ISBN 978-1-4555-8962-3 (large print hardcover) —
ISBN (invalid) 978-1-4789-0383-3 (audiobook) — ISBN 978-1-4789-0384-0 (audio download) —
ISBN 978-1-4555-3234-6 (spanish ebook) — ISBN 978-1-4555-8781-0 (ebook) — ISBN
978-1-4555-3235-3 (spanish trade pbk.)   1. God (Christianity)—Worship and love.
2. Spiritual warfare. 3. Spiritual life—Christianity. I. Title.
    BV4817.M495 2015
    248.4—dc23
                                      2014049888

CONTENTS

You shall not need to fight in this battle; take your positions, stand still, and see the deliverance of the Lord [Who is] with you, O Judah and Jerusalem. Fear not nor be dismayed. Tomorrow go out against them, for the Lord is with you.

2 Chronicles 20:17

All of us face various kinds of battles in our lives. No one escapes problems and challenges, which we often call "the storms of life." The good news is that God already knows what He will do when we face difficulties; He has a plan to bring us victory. Second Chronicles 20 tells us that we do not need to fight our own battles because our battles belong to the Lord, not to us. All we need to do is take our position and remain in them until our breakthroughs come.

What is our position? I believe it is worshipping God.

Unless we have a strong faith in God, anytime a storm comes into our lives, the first thing that happens is that we lose our peace and begin to feel fear. Our enemy, Satan, injects "what if" thoughts into our heads, and we often begin to think we will have the worst possible outcome. As soon as this happens, we should realize what is going on: The enemy is trying to keep us from going forward in God's will and experiencing His good plans for our lives. God wants us to be totally free from fear. He does not want us to live in torment, and He does not want fear to stop us from confidently doing what He leads us to do. When we have a deep understanding of God's perfect unconditional love for us, we realize He will always take care of everything that concerns us. That knowledge eventually delivers us from fear. As we gain experience with God and see that He always takes care of us and provides what we need, we begin to relax.

> *There is no fear in love [dread does not exist], but full-grown (complete, perfect) love turns fear out of doors and expels every trace of terror! For fear brings with it the thought of punishment, and [so] he who is afraid has not reached the full maturity of love [is not yet grown into love's complete perfection].*
>
> 1 John 4:18

God moves on our behalf when we focus on Him instead of on our fears. Thoughts or feelings of fear are nothing more than the enemy's attempts to distract us from God and His will for our lives. We may feel fear at various times in our lives, but we can trust God. And if we need to do something, even though we feel afraid, we can do it. This "do it afraid" theory is something God began teaching me many years ago. I saw that when He told Joshua to "fear not" (Joshua 8:1), He was actually warning him that fear would try to stop him from moving ahead with God's plan for his life; instead of letting fear control him, he needed to be strong and full of courage and to keep going forward. He needed to fight and win the battle against fear so he could experience the victory of fulfilling God's plan and enjoy everything God had for him.

> *For God has not given us a spirit of fear, but of power and of love and of a sound mind.*
>
> 2 Timothy 1:7 NKJV

When we feel fear or begin to have fearful thoughts, the first thing we should do is pray. I often say, "Pray about everything and fear nothing." We should set ourselves to seek God until we know we have overcome our fears mentally and emotionally. As we seek God, we are focusing on Him instead of on our fears. We worship Him for Who He is and express our appreciation for the good He has done, is doing, and will continue to do.

God has new opportunities and great things in store for us. To receive them, we will need to take steps of faith. That often means doing things we don't feel like doing or may not even think will work. Our trust and reverence for God must be greater than what we think, want, or feel.

The enemy brings all kinds of storms into our lives. He also tries to use fear in many different forms to keep us from experiencing everything God has for us. Even though we may feel fear, we need to focus our attention on God. He has a battle plan for us, and He will give us courage and faith to receive the peace, victories, and blessings He has for us.

In this book, you will read a lot about both praise and worship, and you might wonder what the difference is. I believe one of the ways to explain it is to say that we praise God for all of His mighty acts, and we worship Him for Who He is. If our lives are filled with plenty of both, we will see God fight our battles for us and we will experience joyful victories.

PART I

GOD'S BATTLE PLAN

CHAPTER I

Phase I:
Hear Directly from God

In 2 Chronicles 20:1, several types of "-ites" came against King Jehoshaphat and the people of Judah—the Moabites, the Ammonites, and the Meunites. In other places in the Old Testament, the Jebusites, the Hittites, and the Canaanites were the troublemakers for God's people. Today, as Christians, we face the other kinds of "-ites"—the fear-ites, disease-ites, stress-ites, poverty-ites, bad marriage-ites, grouchy neighbor-ites, insecurity-ites, rejection-ites, and others.

So let me ask you: Are the "-ites" after you? How many things are coming against you right now? To help you know how to deal with them, let's look at what King

Jehoshaphat did when faced with his enemies. He turned his attention to God instead of focusing on all the "-ites" that were trying to defeat him, destroy him, and take over his kingdom.

> *It was told Jehoshaphat, A great multitude has come against you from beyond the [Dead] Sea, from Edom; and behold, they are in Hazazon-tamar, which is En-gedi. Then Jehoshaphat feared, and set himself [determinedly, as his vital need] to seek the Lord; he proclaimed a fast in all Judah.*
>
> 2 Chronicles 20:2–3

When Jehoshaphat heard the "-ites" were coming against him, the first thing he did was fear. But then he did something else: He set himself to seek the Lord. Determined to hear from God, he even proclaimed a fast throughout the land for that very purpose. He knew he needed to hear from God. He needed a battle plan, and only God could give him one guaranteed to succeed.

Phase 1 of God's battle plan is to combat fear by hearing from God. Romans 10:17 teaches us that "faith comes by hearing, and hearing by the word of God" (NKJV). This verse is not referring to the written Word of God, but to the spoken word of God, called *rhema* in Greek (the original language of the New Testament). In other words, when we hear God's word, faith fills our hearts and drives fear away. Jehoshaphat knew he had to hear from God, and you and I have the same need.

God may speak to us by giving us peace deep inside, giving us a creative idea, calming our troubled emotions, or filling our hearts with the calm assurance that everything is going to be okay in a certain situation. In 1989, I needed to hear God in these ways.

I went to the doctor for a regular checkup. He discovered a small lump in my breast and wanted me to have a biopsy immediately. I did not think it would be anything serious, but the test showed a fast-growing type of cancer, and the doctors highly recommended immediate surgery.

I remember walking down the hallway in my house, with fear hitting me so strongly I felt I was going to fall to the floor. My knees actually felt they were about to buckle under me. Every night when I went to bed, I had a hard time going to sleep. When I did sleep, it was not a good, restful sleep; it was fitful. Every so often, I woke up, and when I did, fears were pounding at my mind.

Cancer is a word that usually brings great fear. No matter how many friends or family members told me God would take care of it, I still battled fear until early one morning, about 3:00 A.M., God spoke deep in my heart and gave me assurance that He would take care of me. After that, I did not experience that sickening, crippling feeling of fear again.

After my surgery, I was apprehensive as I waited for the results of tests on my lymph nodes to see if I would need further treatment, but I still knew I was in God's hands, and whatever happened, He would take care of me.

As it turned out, I did not need any further

treatment. We actually realized that, through early detection, God had saved my life. I ended up thankful instead of fearful.

Look to God, Not to a Method

When Jehoshaphat heard a huge army was amassing against Judah, he knew what to do and what not to do. He did not seek advice from other people—friends, family members, or even brilliant military advisors; he was determined to hear from God.

Jehoshaphat had probably been involved in other battles previously, so why didn't he just use some of the same methods he had used before? No matter how many times something has worked in the past, it may not solve a current crisis unless God empowers it in a fresh, new way. He may allow an old method to be effective, but He may also give us direction we have never had before. We must always look to God, not to methods.

God does use methods, but they have no power unless He works through them.

Focusing on a method is just as unwise and ineffective as focusing on our fears. Our focus, our source of supply, must be God—and God alone. Our answers are not in methods; they are in relationship with God.

Jehoshaphat knew that unless he heard from God, he would be defeated. That need to hear from the Lord is what the *Amplified Bible* calls his "vital need" (2 Chronicles 20:3). Some things we can do without; others are vital and necessary. Jehoshaphat knew God's direction was vital.

You may be in a situation similar to Jehoshaphat's. You, too, may need a word or clear leading from God. You may feel that, like a drowning person, you are going under for the last time. You may desperately need a word from the Lord if you are going to survive.

Be encouraged. God wants to speak to you even more than you want to hear from Him. Seek Him, not a method, by giving Him your time and attention, and you will not be disappointed.

Show God You're Sincere

Jehoshaphat proclaimed a fast in all Judah, and the people gathered to seek the Lord for help, yearning for Him with all their desire.

And Judah gathered together to ask help from the Lord; even out of all the cities of Judah they came to seek the Lord [yearning for Him with all their desire]. And Jehoshaphat stood in the assembly of Judah and Jerusalem in the house of the Lord before the new court and said, O Lord, God of our fathers, are You not God in heaven?

2 Chronicles 20:4–6

Jehoshaphat proclaimed a fast to show his sincerity to God. When we have a problem, it is good to spend extra time with God, perhaps using the time we would spend eating or watching television to pray and seek God's wisdom. Instead of spending an evening with friends telling them all about your troubles and asking for their advice, use that time to go to God first. These types of actions show that you know hearing from God is vital. I have learned that to seek means to pursue, crave, and go after something with all your might. In other words, a person who seeks is like a starving man in search of food to keep himself alive. The process of seeking is that intense.

Talk to God About Himself

Instead of immediately presenting his problem to the Lord, Jehoshaphat began to talk to the Lord about how mighty He is. He turned his focus to the Lord instead of keeping it on his problem.

> *O Lord, God of our fathers, are You not God in heaven? And do You not rule over all the kingdoms of the nations? In Your hand are power and might, so that none is able to withstand You.*
>
> 2 Chronicles 20:6

Instead of talking to God only about our problems, we need to talk to Him about Himself—about Who He is, about the power of His name and the power of the blood of His Son Jesus, about the great things He has done and what He can do. After we have praised and worshipped Him this way, we can begin to mention our troubles. We should enter God's presence with thanksgiving and come into His courts with praise (see Psalm 100:4).

When I think about this, I think of my children. I wouldn't want them to run in the front door and tell me what they need without even saying, "Hello, Mom, how are you?" I would not want them to only spend time with me or pay attention to me when they had problems. I want them to fellowship with me often. The same principle applies to us with God. We don't want to be people who seek Him only when we are in trouble, but we need to fellowship with Him all the time.

God called Abraham His friend. That's who I want to be too—a person who spends time with Him when things are going well and when they are not. The Lord is not just our problem solver; He is our everything, and we need to relate to Him that way.

"Now, Lord, Behold Our Problem"

If we pay attention to what the Lord is saying through 2 Chronicles 20:7–11, we will learn something that will change our battle plan. It will give us a new way of dealing with our problems for the rest of our lives and make a way for victory after victory.

> *Did not You, O our God, drive out the inhabitants of this land before Your people Israel and give it forever to the descendants of Abraham Your friend? They dwelt in it and have built You a sanctuary in it for Your Name, saying, If evil comes upon us, the sword of judgment, or pestilence, or famine, we will stand before this house and before You— for Your Name [and the symbol of Your presence] is in this house—and cry to*

*You in our affliction, and You will hear
and save. And now behold, the men of
Ammon, Moab, and Mount Seir, whom
You would not let Israel invade when they
came from the land of Egypt, and whom
they turned from and did not destroy—
behold, they reward us by coming to drive
us out of Your possession which You have
given us to inherit.*

2 Chronicles 20:7–11

After starting his prayer by acknowledging how great, awesome, powerful, and wonderful the Lord is, Jehoshaphat began relating specific mighty acts God had performed in the past to protect His people and to uphold His promises to them. And in finally presenting his request, he began by expressing his confidence that the Lord would handle the problem. Jehoshaphat said basically, "Oh, by the way, our enemies are coming against us to try to take away the possession for our inheritance. I just thought I would mention this little problem. But You are so great, I know You already have it all under control."

I have often heard that our praises should outnumber our petitions, and I totally agree.

We can and should always ask God for what we need, but I don't think all of our prayer time should be filled with what we need. We should always include praise, worship, thanksgiving, and intercession for others.

God has a plan for our deliverance before our problems ever appear. He is not surprised when trouble comes. He is not in Heaven wringing His hands trying to figure out what to do. He's in control. Our part is to focus on Him and His mighty power, worshipping Him and praising Him for the manifestation of His solution and listening for a word of direction from Him.

CHAPTER 2

Phase 2:
Admit Your Dependence
on God

O our God, will You not exercise judgment upon them? For we have no might to stand against this great company that is coming against us. We do not know what to do, but our eyes are upon You.

2 Chronicles 20:12

Phase 2 of God's battle plan for Jehoshaphat is found in 2 Chronicles 20:12. Here Jehoshaphat admitted to God openly his total inability to deal with the problem.

Like Jehoshaphat, we also need to realize we cannot solve the problems we face in life. We do not have answers to every question. We do not know how to deal with every situation we encounter. We are not much different from Jehoshaphat in that there are times when we just don't know what to do. Instead of spinning our wheels trying to figure out what to do about things we cannot do anything about until we are completely frustrated and totally exhausted from struggling, we need to let God do for us what we cannot do for ourselves.

For years, I tried hard to change myself without success. I tried so hard for so long to break bad habits, only to fail time and time again. I tried to alter different things in my life, to make my ministry grow and to be healed. I was constantly battling against the "-ites." I remember wanting to give up simply because I was so exhausted from trying to fight my own battles.

I kept trying, without success, on a regular basis until one day I become kind of melodramatic about it, trying to impress God with how miserable I was. I said something like, "God, I've had it. This is it. I'm finished. Nothing I'm doing is working. I give up. I'm not going to do this anymore."

Just then, in my heart, I sensed the Holy Spirit was saying, "Really?"

It was almost as though He was excited. Maybe that was because, so often, the only time He gets to work in us is when we become so exhausted that we finally decide we will surrender everything to God.

Trying to do what only God can do will wear you out fast. Why not give up your own effort and follow Jehoshaphat's example? Admit to God that you have no might to stand against your enemies and you don't know what to do, but you are looking to Him for direction and deliverance.

Three things Jehoshaphat did were very important. First, he acknowledged he had no might to stand against his enemies. Second, he admitted he did not know what to do. And third, he said his eyes were on God. By saying these three things, Jehoshaphat put himself in position for a miracle.

Total Dependence on God

Jesus said, "Apart from me you can do nothing" (John 15:5 NIV). The first time I read this verse, I had not even begun to realize how true it is. I was a very independent person, and God began highlighting this Scripture to me early in my walk with Him. One of the keys to receiving anything from God is entire dependence on Him. Without faith, we cannot please God (see Hebrews 11:6). Faith is the channel through which we receive from Him, and the *Amplified Bible* describes faith as the leaning of the entire human personality in absolute trust "in His power, wisdom, and goodness" (2 Timothy 1:5).

We are to lean on, rely only, and depend entirely on God, taking all the weight of our problems and burdens off ourselves and putting it all on Him. Think of it this way: When I plop down in a big easy chair, I am putting my entire dependence on that chair to hold me. I take all the weight off myself and put it all on the chair. It is amazing that we trust a chair more than we do God many times. We often say we lean on God, and perhaps we do partially, but we have difficulty leaning *entirely* on Him. We often have a backup plan just in case God does not come through.

Let's recap what we know thus far about how Jehoshaphat got direction to fight his battle when the "-ites" came against him. We know he set himself to seek God and that he even began to fast. We know he started talking to God about His amazing goodness and faithfulness. And we know he did not mention the problem he had to God until *after* he had praised and worshipped Him. After he had done those things, he openly admitted his entire dependence on God. He said what we often have a hard time saying: "I don't know what to do."

Jehoshaphat did not feel weak or inadequate when he did not know what to do, and neither should we. He told God, "We don't know what to do, and even if we did, we wouldn't have the strength to do it." By saying this and meaning it, he put himself in a position of total dependence on God. He did this early in the battle, teaching us that the sooner we rely on God entirely, the sooner our victory will come.

Without God's help, we can't change anything in our lives. We can't change ourselves, our spouses, our families, our friends, or our circumstances. Truly, apart from God, we cannot do anything that will have lasting value and be done correctly.

We often try to figure out things we have no business even touching with our minds, and we forfeit peace and joy by not giving God total control over our lives. Some things are simply too difficult for us to understand, but nothing is too hard for God. God is infinite, but we are finite human beings with limitations. God has surpassing knowledge, but ours is limited (see 1 Corinthians 13:9). We know some things, but we don't know everything. There are some things we just need to leave alone. We won't ever know everything, but we can grow to a place where we are satisfied to know the One who does know. When we arrive at that place, we enter God's rest, which also releases joy in our lives.

One of the most liberating things we can say is, "Lord, I don't know what to do, and even if I did, I couldn't do it without You. But Lord, my eyes are on You. I am going to wait and watch for You to do something about this situation, because there is absolutely nothing I can do about it unless You give me direction."

When we are faced with difficult or impossible situations, the enemy may whisper over and over in our minds, "What are you going to do? What are you going to do?" Our friends may say, "I heard about your situation. What are you going to do?"

These are the times when we should say, "I'm going to do what Jehoshaphat did. I'm going to turn it over to the Lord—and wait on Him. He will do something wonderful, and I am going to enjoy watching Him do it!"

Wait on the Lord

And all Judah stood before the Lord, with their children and their wives.

2 Chronicles 20:13

I believe 2 Chronicles 20:13 is a "power verse" when we apply it to our lives. Standing still is action from God's perspective—spiritual action. We usually take action in the natural realm and do nothing spiritually, but in waiting on God and standing before Him, Jehoshaphat took spiritual action. He was basically saying, "Lord, I am going to wait on You until You do something about this situation. In the meantime, I am going to enjoy my life while I am waiting on You to move."

Enjoying life while we are waiting on God to move is not being irresponsible. Jesus said, "The thief comes only in order to steal and kill and destroy. I came that they may have and enjoy life, and have it in abundance (to the full, till it overflows)" (John 10:10).

We are tempted to think we are not doing our part if we don't worry or try to figure out some kind of answer. We must resist that temptation because it prevents our deliverance rather than aiding it.

Faced with an overwhelming force

descending upon them to enslave them and destroy their land, all of Judah came and stood before the Lord. Meanwhile, I am sure the devil was attacking with thoughts of, "What are you going to do? What are you going to do?"

But they just stood, waiting on God.

Isaiah 40:31 says, "They that wait upon the Lord shall renew their strength; they shall mount up with wings as eagles; they shall run, and not be weary; and they shall walk, and not faint" (KJV). We may need the strength we gain while waiting in order to do whatever God will instruct us to do when He gives us direction. Those who wait on the Lord are the ones who receive answers and the ones who are strong enough to follow God's direction once they have it.

Waiting for Answers

Then the Spirit of the Lord came upon Jahaziel son of Zechariah, the son of Benaiah, the son of Jeiel, the son of Mattaniah, a Levite of the sons of Asaph, in

the midst of the assembly. He said, Hear-
ken, all Judah, you inhabitants of Jeru-
salem, and you King Jehoshaphat. The
Lord says this to you: Be not afraid or
dismayed at this great multitude; for the
battle is not yours, but God's.

2 Chronicles 20:14–15

When all of Judah was assembled before the Lord, someone began to prophesy. The Spirit of God came on him and spoke through him because the people were waiting on God to lead them.

When we learn to seek God and wait on Him, He will give us an answer. That answer may be very plain and simple. The Lord told Judah not to be afraid because the battle was His. That does not sound too mystical or deeply spiritual, but it was all they needed to hear.

What good news God's answer must have been to Jehoshaphat and the people: "The battle is not yours, but God's." That did not mean they did not have to do anything; it meant God would show them their part.

They could do it in God's strength and wisdom, but the battle was still His to win.

After that word of encouragement came a word of instruction, as we will see. We are to wait on the Lord until He has told us what we are to do—and then we are to do it in His strength, which we have gained while waiting on Him.

CHAPTER 3

Phase 3:
Take Your Position

Tomorrow go down to them. Behold, they will come up by the Ascent of Ziz, and you will find them at the end of the ravine before the Wilderness of Jeruel. You shall not need to fight in this battle; take your positions, stand still, and see the deliverance of the Lord [Who is] with you, O Judah and Jerusalem. Fear not nor be dismayed....

2 Chronicles 20:16–17

Second Chronicles 20:16–17 tells the people of Judah what position to take for the battle. I always thought their position—and ours—was to stand still. Although that is true, another position was equally important to them. After receiving this instruction from the Lord, Jehoshaphat bowed on his knees with his face to the ground and worshipped (see verse 18). Wow! Worship was their actual position, and in worshipping they would also be standing still. The reverent position of being on our knees with our faces bowed to the ground is a battle posture. Kneeling with uplifted hands is a position from which to fight and gain victory.

David said of God that He "teaches my hands to war and my fingers to fight" (Psalm 144:1). I believe he was taught to lift his hands in worship and surrender to the Lord, and he recognized this as a battle position. Perhaps when David played his musical instruments, his fingers were fighting. Praise, worship, clapping our hands in enthusiasm, singing, God's Word, joy—all of these are weapons of warfare.

We Don't Have Worldly Weapons

For the weapons of our warfare are not physical [weapons of flesh and blood], but they are mighty before God for the overthrow and destruction of strongholds.
                                                2 Corinthians 10:4

Our weapons are not natural, earthly weapons. They are not tools the natural mind would understand or things that might even seem to work in the physical realm. But in God's Kingdom, they do work. When the Israelites were in battle, they often sent the tribe of Judah ahead of everyone else. Why? Because Judah represents praise. They entered into their warfare with worshippers going before them.

Like the Israelites, we must learn to fight our battles God's way, not the world's way. Ephesians 6:12 says: "We wrestle not against flesh and blood, but against principalities, against powers, against the rulers of the darkness of this world, against spiritual wickedness in high places" (KJV). In other words, the battles we fight are not against people (flesh and blood); they are against Satan, the enemy of our souls. Therefore, spiritually speaking, we take the battle position of standing our ground and worshipping the Lord.

Ephesians 6:13–14 says: "Therefore put on God's complete armor, that you may be able to resist and stand your ground on the evil day [of danger], and, having done all [the crisis demands], to stand [firmly in your place]. Stand therefore [hold your ground]..."

To *stand* means to abide in or to enter God's rest—not necessarily physical rest, but spiritual rest. When I am standing my ground, I am refusing to give in. I am persisting in believing that God will deliver me. I am abiding (remaining and continuing) in Him.

In battles against our spiritual enemies, our position is in Christ. It is abiding and resting in Him, in worship and praise. When you are faced with a crisis and don't know what to do, follow the instructions God gave

Jehoshaphat and his people: Take your position (worship); stand still and see the salvation of the Lord. Calm down, stop trying to figure out the answers, and turn your focus to God. Open your mouth and sing the songs of worship that are in your heart. Psalm 32:7 says God will give us songs of deliverance, but we must sing them in order for them to be effective against the forces of evil.

Worshipping God is not only for times when we come together in church services; it is something we need to do privately too, in our everyday lives. We cannot always bow down, lift our hands, or sing aloud; sometimes those things would be inappropriate. But in our hearts we can always worship—anytime, anyplace.

Bow Down, Stand Up, Praise God

And Jehoshaphat bowed his head with his face to the ground, and all Judah and the inhabitants of Jerusalem fell down before the Lord, worshiping Him. And some

Levites of the Kohathites and Korahites stood up to praise the Lord, the God of Israel, with a very loud voice.

2 Chronicles 20:18–19

Let's get a picture of what happened in this situation. First, everyone bowed down to worship the Lord—a position of humility before Him. Then, some of them stood and started praising God with very loud voices.

I believe bowing down before the Lord is something we need to do on a regular basis, as is standing to praise Him. We do not need to get caught up in postures or positions, but we do need to worship God consistently, because we believe He deserves our worship and because our hearts are filled with love and reverence toward Him.

If you have a business that is struggling financially and you are in a situation where you just don't know what to do, I recommend going into your office, closing the door, getting on your knees, lifting your hands, and thanking God that He is good and that He is taking care of your problems. You can even do this several times a day, especially when you begin to feel overwhelmed.

Believe and Remain Steadfast

And they rose early in the morning and went out into the Wilderness of Tekoa; and as they went out, Jehoshaphat stood and said, Hear me, O Judah, and you inhabitants of Jerusalem! Believe in the Lord your God and you shall be established; believe and remain steadfast to His prophets and you shall prosper.

2 Chronicles 20:20

After the people worshipped and praised the Lord, they went out to meet the enemy. Notice that they went out to face their adversary *after* they had worshipped and praised, not before.

As they went out, Jehoshaphat reminded them of the word of the Lord that came forth the day before and told them not to start doubting it. Some of us may also need to go back to something the Lord has impressed upon us in the past. God can give us words of comfort or direction, and we can be very excited, filled with faith, feeling bold and able to conquer the enemy. Yet we can also forget that word, especially if it seems to take a long time to come to pass, and when that happens, we need to return to it. For example, the New Testament tells the story of a time when Timothy became fearful and discouraged, and Paul encouraged him to remember the words of prophecy given to him at the time of his ordination (see 1 Timothy 4:14; 2 Timothy 1:6–7).

Jehoshaphat told the people to believe the prophets, to remember the word the prophet had given the previous day, which was: "The battle is not yours, but God's." The enemy will whisper all kinds of lies to you, but God's Word is truth. Go to His written Word or to a personal word He has spoken to your heart at some time, and remember that God cannot lie. His promises are sure, and you can depend on them. Remain steadfast in your belief, and you will be delivered.

Sing, Praise, and Give Thanks

*When he had consulted with the people,
he appointed singers to sing to the Lord
and praise Him in their holy [priestly]
garments as they went out before the
army, saying, Give thanks to the Lord,
for His mercy and loving-kindness endure
forever!*

2 Chronicles 20:21

Second Chronicles 20:21 shows us the
essence of God's battle plan for Jehoshaphat
and his people—and for us: Sing to the Lord,
praise Him, and give thanks to Him. As they
went out to battle, the people offering praise
said, "Give thanks to the Lord, for His mercy
and loving-kindness endure forever!"

Singing and giving thanks may not seem
like the thing to do in times of trouble, but
believe me, it is exactly what we need to
do. Many things do not make sense to our
minds, but that does not mean we should not
do them. We rely on our minds far too much
without realizing that many wrong things

are programmed into our thought patterns from years of operating in the world's system. Romans 12:2 states that we need to renew our minds by God's Word in order to experience His good will for our lives.

Let me give you an example of how effective singing praise to God can be during a difficult situation.

Years ago, I was having some severe headaches, so the doctor wrote me a prescription. The medicine made me feel like a freight train was going through my head. I actually had a loud roar in my head that made me feel as though I was going crazy.

I took the medicine for one day, and that night, I could not sleep. I was sick to my stomach, I had the roaring pain in my head, and the enemy was lying to me. My family line had included some mental illness, and Satan was taking advantage of that, telling me I was losing my mind. While all of this was happening to me at about two in the morning, my husband, Dave, was sound asleep. The house was very quiet, and I felt completely alone with my pain. I felt I was going to be sick, so I got out of bed and headed for the bathroom.

Sitting on the bathroom floor with the side of my head and face resting on the toilet seat, I sensed unmistakably that the Holy Spirit was saying, "Sing."

Sing? I thought.

I didn't feel like singing. I felt like throwing up, maybe even giving up—anything but standing up and singing. However, the instruction persisted: "Sing."

I felt depressed, like crying, feeling sorry for myself and even getting angry with Dave for sleeping while I was suffering. But I knew that if I truly expected a breakthrough from God, I needed to obey Him and not act on my feelings.

As I thought about what to sing, I thought of an old hymn I had not heard in many years, "In the Garden." It reminded me of Jesus and how He suffered in the Garden of Gethsemane. Surely, if He could make it, so could I. In obedience to God, I opened my mouth and began to croak out the song.

Before too long, I began to feel better and was able to go to bed and go to sleep.

I hope this example encourages you to sing to God when trouble comes. Jehoshaphat may have felt like I did on the bathroom floor—miserable and maybe even wanting to give up—but he was obedient to God, and that was a key to his success over the enemy.

Just Worship

When we have needs in our lives, we can worship God in the midst of them rather than begging Him to meet them. James 4:2 says there are things we do not have because we do not ask God for them. So we need to make our requests known, but we do not need to get into a pleading mode. We are believers, not beggars.

Matthew 6 teaches us that when we pray, we are not to repeat the same phrases over and over, thinking God will hear us if we speak enough. Quality is much more important than quantity. We often have the mistaken idea that if prayers are long, they are effective, but that is not true. I explain this in detail in my book *The Power of Simple Prayer.*

I believe we can sometimes say so much to God that we are not even sure what we are asking for. I can remember times when I actually found myself talking so much when I prayed that I got confused. Several years ago, God was dealing with me about this and challenged me to begin asking Him very simply for what I wanted and needed, using the fewest words possible. This required me to learn a new discipline, but I began to do it. Then, I used the remainder of my time to wait in God's presence or simply worship Him. I found this way of praying to be much more refreshing and effective for me than talking so much. I sometimes still catch myself slipping back into my old ways, thinking more words are better, and the Lord has to remind me again that simplicity is powerful.

I feel the best way to see our needs met

is to ask for what we need and then worship God because *He* is what we need. He does not just give us what we need; He Himself is everything we need. When we need peace, He is our peace. When we need to know we are cleansed, righteous, and not guilty before Him, He is our righteousness. When we need joy and strength, He is our joy and His joy gives us strength.

I have noticed that when I worship God for one of His attributes, I see that attribute released in my life. If we need mercy, we should begin to worship and praise God for His mercy. If we need provision or finances, we should begin to worship and praise God that He has already promised that we will never lack any good thing (see Psalm 84:11). Whatever you need, the best thing to do is pray, praise, and worship God. As your need comes to mind through the days and weeks ahead, thank God that He has heard your prayer and is working on your situation. Thank Him that good things are on the way.

Release Through Worship

Sometimes we are under so much mental or emotional pressure that we feel we just need some kind of release. Worship brings that release. As we worship the Lord, we release the mental or emotional burdens that weigh us down. They seem to fade away as we focus on the awesomeness of God.

I encourage you to begin to worship early in the morning, even before you get out of bed. Worship while you get ready for your day and while you drive to work. If you do this, you will be amazed at how things will change at home and on the job because of the way God begins to work. Worship focuses on Who God is, His character, goodness, faithfulness, grace, love, and many other wonderful things.

Murmuring, grumbling, faultfinding, or being negative all create an atmosphere in which the enemy can work. But worship does the opposite; it creates an atmosphere in which God can work.

Worship transforms us. By starting to

worship God for the changes He is already working in us, we find that those changes start manifesting more and more, and we experience new levels of God's presence, power, and goodness in our lives. As we worship, we remain in position to receive these things and everything else God has for us.

CHAPTER 4

Phase 4:
The Lord Brings Deliverance

And when they began to sing and to praise, the Lord set ambushments against the men of Ammon, Moab, and Mount Seir who had come against Judah, and they were [self-] slaughtered.

2 Chronicles 20:22

Second Chronicles 20:22 says that while the people of Judah sang praise to God, He set ambushes against their enemies, and the enemies slaughtered themselves. Praise confused the enemy.

This is great news! The people of God were determined to seek Him rather than live in fear. They told God how awesome He is; they stood and waited on Him. He sent a prophet with a word for them, letting them know the battle was not theirs, but His. He told them to take their position and stand still. They worshipped and praised. Jehoshaphat appointed singers to sing and praise, and the Lord defeated their enemies by confusing them so much that they killed each other!

In the book of Judges, we see another example of God's deliverance through a battle plan that would not seem to work in the natural realm.

Then Jerubbaal, that is, Gideon, and all the people who were with him rose early and encamped beside the spring of Harod; and the camp of Midian was north of them by the hill of Moreh in the valley. The Lord said to Gideon, The people who are with you are too many for Me to give the Midianites into their hands, lest Israel boast about themselves against Me, saying, My own hand has delivered me. So now proclaim in the ears of the men, saying, Whoever is fearful and trembling, let him turn back and depart from Mount Gilead. And 22,000 of the men returned, but 10,000 remained.

Judges 7:1–3

Gideon was facing a major battle, but instead of telling him that He would give him more men, God told him he had too many for God to give him the victory. Sometimes God works through our weaknesses instead of through our strengths. There are times when we have too much going for us from a natural perspective for God to work a miracle. We do not need God's intervention if anyone but God can help us. When God told Gideon he had too many men, He was letting him know that they were too strong in themselves; He wanted them in a position where they had to depend on Him entirely.

Let the Fearful Go Home

God instructed Gideon to tell everyone who was fearful to go home. Twenty-two thousand of them left; ten thousand stayed to face the enemy. This tells us more men were afraid than were not afraid. How many times does God put something in our hearts to do, but then fear comes along and we hesitate and become double-minded? God says, "Fear not, for I am with you" (Isaiah 41:10 NKJV). The fact that God is with us is the number one reason we do not have to give in to fear and let it control our future. God is with us and will protect us if we put our trust in Him.

> And the Lord said to Gideon, The men are still too many; bring them down to the water, and I will test them for you there. And he of whom I say to you, This man shall go with you, shall go with you; and he of whom I say to you, This man shall not go with you, shall not go. So he brought the men down to the water, and the Lord said to Gideon, Everyone who laps up the water with his tongue as a dog laps it, you shall set by himself; likewise everyone who bows down on his knees to drink. And the number of those

who lapped, putting their hand to their mouth, was 300 men, but all the rest of the people bowed down upon their knees to drink water. And the Lord said to Gideon, With the 300 men who lapped I will deliver you, and give the Midianites into your hand. Let all the others return every man to his home.

Judges 7:4–7

When I first read this passage, I wondered what all the lapping and bowing was about, so I asked the Lord to help me understand. He led me to a footnote in a Bible I rarely use, and the note explained this incident.

The scenario went something like this: The men were all thirsty. When they saw the water, some of them ran to it, bowed down on their knees, put their faces in the water, and began to drink. Others cupped their hands and brought the water to their mouths. Those who cupped their hands were still able to look around and watch for the enemy while they were drinking. They remained alert and ready to do their job while the others focused only on satisfying their thirst and did not pay attention to what was happening around them. They were so emotional about getting their thirst quenched that they missed the chance to be part of God's miracle.

Like these soldiers, we can stay so busy trying to provide for ourselves that we miss God's will. The 300 who cupped their hands showed wisdom, diligence, and the willingness to be aware of their surroundings, on the lookout for the enemy while still getting the water they needed. These are the type of people through whom God chooses to work.

Keep Your Eyes on God

So the people took provisions and their trumpets in their hands, and he sent all the rest of Israel every man to his home and retained those 300 men. And the host of Midian was below him in the valley. That same night the Lord said to Gideon, Arise, go down against their camp, for I have given it into your hand. But if you fear to go down, go with Purah your servant down to the camp and you shall hear what they say, and afterward your hands shall be strengthened to go down against the camp. Then he went down with Purah his servant to the outposts of the camp of the armed men. And the Midianites and the Amalekites and all the sons of the east lay along the valley like locusts for multitude; and their camels were without number, as the sand on the seashore for multitude. When Gideon arrived, behold, a man was telling a dream to his comrade. And he said, Behold, I dreamed a dream, and behold, a cake of barley bread tumbled into the camp of Midian and came to the tent and struck it so that it fell, and turned it upside down so that the tent lay flat.

Judges 7:8–13

Here Gideon again received the direction he needed from God, this time through a dream. Gideon needed such an encouraging word because he had started with an army of 32,000 men and was now down to only 300. The enemy army was so big they looked like the sands of the sea. This dream let Gideon know his small army would not defeat their enemy through natural means, but God would give them victory in a supernatural way.

When I studied this passage, I learned that barley bread was considered inferior in some ways to bread made with "fine flour." But in Gideon's dream the barley bread was sufficient to bring victory. God showed Gideon that something as insignificant as a barley cake could be used to flatten the enemy's camp, so Gideon could be used by God too. The Lord was not trying to insult Gideon; He was simply trying to get him in the same position we all need to be in—knowing that he could do nothing without God. This story should encourage us that, like Gideon, we do not need what the world considers the best resources to win our battles. All we need to do is keep our eyes on God.

I recall driving to one of my weekly

meetings a few years ago, and it had been raining very hard all day and wasn't stopping. I had been praying diligently for the rain to stop, but it continued to rain. God whispered to my heart, "Would it be a greater miracle for Me to stop the rain, or fill the house in the midst of it?" We had a full house that night and I was amazed!

Recently I was at an event in Tulsa, Oklahoma. It was a huge outreach to the poor and needy in the city, and I had been asked to speak. The event was held in a minor league baseball stadium, and my podium was at home plate. It was also raining that day, and in order for the people to attend, they were going to get wet unless they had umbrellas, and most of them didn't. I was going to get wet also, but I was willing to do that if the people came. God reminded me of the other time He filled the house in the midst of the rain, and I trusted that He could do it again. Ten thousand people showed up, and we still had a very successful outreach to the needy people there.

Bad circumstances don't stop God. He can deliver by many or by few, and He can have success in dry weather or rain.

When Gideon's comrades returned, they knew God had spoken, and after sharing the good news with Gideon, they worshipped.

Get the Word and Worship

And his comrade replied, This is nothing else but the sword of Gideon son of Joash, a man of Israel. Into his hand God has given Midian and all the host. When Gideon heard the telling of the dream and its interpretation, he worshiped and returned to the camp of Israel and said, Arise, for the Lord has given into your hand the host of Midian.

Judges 7:14–15

As soon as Gideon received this personal direction from God, he began to talk about the battle as though it were already won. He began to praise and worship God as though the victory had already been accomplished. He did not wait to see the actual results of the battle before he proclaimed the triumph of the Lord.

I am still amazed when I think about how often God uses people who stop to worship Him. This has taught me a great lesson about how to deal with life's battles, and I pray it will have the same effect on you.

In Exodus 14, the Israelites passed through the Red Sea on dry ground while their enemies drowned. Once they had crossed over, they sang praise to God. They were all excited, dancing and playing their tambourines. They sang at length about the greatness of God— *after* they had experienced His power. They sang the right song, but perhaps they sang it on the wrong side of the river.

Failing to praise and worship God after a victory would be very sad, so the fact that the Israelites did acknowledge God's miracle is good. But Gideon did something better as he worshipped God *before* he saw his victory. All he had to do was hear and believe the breakthrough was coming, and he began to praise God. This kind of faith gets God's attention.

Deuteronomy 1:2 tells us that the Israelites' journey through the wilderness to the Promised Land should have taken about eleven days. Instead, it took them forty years. When we look at the Israelites' pattern of worship—*after* God's deliverance—perhaps we begin to understand why they wandered in the wilderness so long in their attempt to make a relatively short journey. They worshipped after seeing a miracle, but most of the time they murmured and complained about their circumstances as they wandered around and around the same mountains. Had they done more singing and worshipping, they might have made it through the wilderness and into the Promised Land much sooner.

We need to follow Gideon's example, not the Israelites' example, and worship God before He acts on our behalf, believing He is for us and trusting Him to win our battles. Worship should come before victory, as well as after it!

Let the Lord Fight the Battle

And he divided the 300 men into three companies, and he put into the hands of all of them trumpets and empty pitchers, with torches inside the pitchers. And he said to them, Look at me, then do likewise. When I come to the edge of their camp, do as I do. When I blow the trumpet, I and all who are with me, then you blow the trumpets also on every side of all the camp and shout, For the Lord and for Gideon! So Gideon and the 100 men who were with him came to the outskirts of the camp at the beginning of the middle watch, when the guards had just been changed, and they blew the trumpets and smashed the pitchers that were in their hands. And the three companies blew the trumpets and shattered the pitchers, holding the torches in their left hands, and in their right hands the trumpets to blow [leaving no chance to use swords], and they cried, The sword for the Lord and Gideon!

Judges 7:16–20

Notice the phrase "leaving no chance to use swords." When God sent Gideon's tiny army to do battle with the vastly superior Midianites, He purposefully put something in both of each man's hands so the men could not help themselves. They could not draw their swords and begin to fight their own battles. God sent 300 men who were fearless and focused on what they were called to do, and they could not fight for themselves. They had to depend on Him completely to fight the battle for them. All they had to do was break a pitcher, hold up a torch, and cry, "The sword for the Lord and Gideon!" In other words, all they had to do was hold the light and praise God.

God's instructions to Gideon were different than they were to Jehoshaphat. Yet His intention was the same—to give them victory. This is why we must seek God and hear Him for ourselves. We cannot just do what someone else did; God leads us individually. He will lead us to what will work for us, not necessarily what worked for someone else.

What Happened

They stood every man in his place round about the camp, and all the [Midianite] army ran—they cried out and fled. When [Gideon's men] blew the 300 trumpets, the Lord set every [Midianite's] sword against his comrade and against all the army, and the army fled...

Judges 7:21–22

The final outcome of Gideon's battle was the same as Jehoshaphat's. When the army of the Lord did what God told them to do, the enemy began to run. Once again, God's battle plan was successful when someone trusted Him and put His plan into action by faith.

PART 2

TRANSFORMED THROUGH WORSHIP

CHAPTER 5

Don't Wrestle, Worship

For we are not wrestling with flesh and blood.

Ephesians 6:12

In waging spiritual warfare, we must remember that we war against our enemy, Satan, and his demons, not against flesh and blood. In other words, we do not fight against people—other people or our own selves.

Perhaps the greatest war we think we wage is with ourselves about ourselves, because the enemy is a master at turning people against themselves. We struggle with where we are spiritually compared to where we need to be. We wrestle with wishing we had accomplished more than we have done in life. We may feel like a failure in our jobs or relationships or in any number of other areas. But one thing is true: We won't change anything by struggling and being frustrated. Only God can fight and win the battles we fight within ourselves.

Getting to the place where we can be honest with ourselves about our sins, failures, and weaknesses, yet still know we are right with God through the righteousness Jesus gives us, is very difficult. What we do is not the same as who we are in Christ.

Many Christians will go to Heaven because they have received salvation, but they will not enjoy their lives on Earth because they do not know how to enjoy God and enjoy themselves. The reason they do not enjoy themselves is that they stay engaged in private internal battles over all their deficiencies. They do not enjoy God because they live with a continual vague feeling that He is displeased with them or even angry with them because of their flaws. They are always wrestling with themselves, always in a war, always struggling.

I once taught a message called "Have You Become a Trial to Yourself?" We often talk about our problems and trials, but frequently our biggest problems are with ourselves. We have more trouble with ourselves than we do with the enemy or with any person on Earth. Sometimes we are our own worst enemy, but there is good news! We can be changed as we worship God and focus on Him—not as we look to ourselves and examine our flaws, but as we look to Him.

We Are Changing

But we all, with open face beholding as in a glass the glory of the Lord, are changed into the same image from glory to glory, even as by the Spirit of the Lord.

2 Corinthians 3:18 *KJV*

Most of us want to change. We want to see changes in our behavior and to make regular progress in the directions in which we want to go. We may want to become more stable or more loving, or we may want to show more of the fruit of the Spirit. We may want to be kind and good to others even when we do not feel like being kind and good or when we have not had a good day.

We cannot do these things on our own, but God has given us the Helper, the Holy Spirit Himself, to help us be like Jesus. Through the power of the Holy Spirit within us, we are able to be sweet, nice, and kind even when things are not going our way. We can stay calm when everything around us seems topsy-turvy, when everything seems to be conspiring against us to cause us to lose our patience and become angry and upset.

Before our youngest son got his driver's license, Dave and I helped him get a car. Of course, he was very eager to be able to drive it as soon as possible. Like many young people, he planned to drive the car the first night he had his license. He wanted to drive to his Bible study group in an area of town far from our house. Dave told him he did not want him driving that night because of the long distance to the Bible study and because it was snowing.

Our son asked if he could take the car out after the Bible study, and we told him he probably could. But when he got home, the snow was falling even harder. Once again, he faced disappointment when we told him he could not drive the car after all because of the weather.

The next morning, the roads were very slippery and it was still snowing. Dave drove to work, then called home to tell our son he *still* could not take the car out. At that point, our son became angry, though I am sure that deep down inside he realized driving in such bad weather was not wise.

I told our son to just stay sweet. "This is only one day in your life," I said. "You will have lots of other days to drive your car."

I tried to tell him that God sometimes tests us, and He uses those tests to stretch our faith. He stretches our capacity to trust Him because He wants to prepare us for future blessings. My encouragement did not seem to help much, but I understood that because I have been in exactly the same place he was many times, and you probably have too.

I share this story because almost all of us become angry when we do not get our way.

Anger is our normal reaction. Our emotions get stirred up, and we begin going in all sorts of directions.

One of my personal goals is to stay sweet, even when I don't get my way. I have improved a lot over the years, but I have to say that I did not make any positive progress until I learned that I could not change myself. I learned that God's love for me was not based on my performance, but on His grace. I learned to go to God and take my position of waiting on and worshipping Him—and learned that He would fight my battles for me.

I needed a great deal of change. I was sexually, mentally, and emotionally abused during my childhood, and I had many problems as a result of being treated that way. I was rebellious toward authority, especially male authority. I had a bad attitude. I didn't trust people. I felt sorry for myself, and I had a chip on my shoulder. Among many other problems, I also felt the world owed me something.

When I look back at my life over the years, I realize I have changed a lot. But it happened little by little, one step at a time. That is how God changes us. He reveals something to us and then waits until we decide to trust Him with it before He works His character in us in that area.

The amount of time required for change depends on several things: (1) how long it takes us to get into agreement with God that we really do have the problem He says we have; (2) how long it takes us to stop making excuses and blaming our problems on other people; (3) how long we spin our wheels, so to speak, trying to change ourselves; and (4) how much time we spend studying God's Word, waiting on and worshipping Him, truly believing He is working in us as we seek Him.

God is always trying to work in us, in our families, and in our circumstances. He is ever present. He calls Himself "I AM" (Exodus 3:14), not "I Was" or "I Will Be," but "I AM." He is present right now and ready to work in our lives. But He will not force His way into our lives; He waits to be invited. As we relax under His mighty hand, He begins to remold us into His original intention for us before we fell under the influence of the world. He will definitely do an excellent job with us if we trust Him and release ourselves into His hand.

Enjoy Your Life

God begins to move as we release our faith. God will even change you as you read this book if you will trust Him to do so. He will take the godly principles in His Word and He will work on both you and your situation while you sit in His presence and enjoy Him.

Some people become consumed by the desire to think of themselves as perfect or to be seen as perfect. They hate themselves every time they make a mistake. Self-hatred and self-rejection become major problems. These attitudes cause problems not only within these people, but also in their relationships with God and with others. All of our relationships begin with how we feel about ourselves. If we do not get along with ourselves, we will not get along with others either. We cannot love and respect ourselves unless we know how much God loves us!

If you are at war with yourself all the time, and you are not enjoying your life, it is a great tragedy. Since we do not wrestle against flesh and blood (see Ephesians 6:12), your war is not really with yourself, but against demonic principalities and powers that have gained strongholds in your life through deceptions in years past. The truth of God's Word uncovers those deceptions on a regular basis as you study and meditate on it. The truth sets us free as we continue in it (see John 8:32).

God changes us from one degree of glory to another (see 2 Corinthians 3:18), little by little, step by step. The important thing to remember about this is to enjoy where you are on the way to where you are headed. Resist the temptation to compare where you are on your journey with someone who seems to be farther along. Each of us is an individual, and God deals with us differently, according to what He knows we need and can handle.

You may not see the changes you want to see on a daily basis, but you can enjoy your life every day, and over the years you will realize that God was indeed changing you little by little. I encourage you to just keep believing that God is working, just as He said He would. When you don't think you are changing, continue to wait on God and worship Him. Continue to believe that He loves you unconditionally. Over time, you will see that He was working in you all along and that you have been transformed into His image.

Our Goal: Christlikeness

For those whom He foreknew [of whom He was aware and loved beforehand], He also destined from the beginning [fore-ordaining them] to be molded into the image of His Son [and share inwardly His likeness], that He might become the firstborn among many brethren.

Romans 8:29

Christlikeness is our number one goal as Christians. Jesus is the "express image" of the Father (Hebrews 1:3 NKJV), and we are to follow in His footsteps. Jesus came as the Pioneer of our faith to show us by example how we should live and conduct ourselves. We should seek to behave and treat other people the way Jesus did. Our goal is not to see how successful we can be in business or some other endeavor, but to be Christlike. This cannot happen unless we learn to let God's grace change us instead of struggling trying to change ourselves. We will respond to God's love by wanting to be like Him.

When we claim to be Christians, we need to have actions that back up our claims. Being forgiving, merciful, and loving are some of the best ways to do so, but that can happen only if we have received God's forgiveness, mercy, and love. Our lives and our godly behavior should make others hungry and thirsty for what we have in Christ. The Bible refers to us as salt, which makes people thirsty, and light, which exposes and leads people out of darkness (see Matthew 5:13–14).

We do not need to be perfect to be effective witnesses for God, but we cannot expect our faith to catch people's attention if we talk about it and then live carnal, fleshly lives.

If we let Him, God will make us better and better as we study His Word. We see Who He is in His written Word, and it becomes as a mirror to us. In other words, when we see ourselves in light of what the Bible says, we realize how we need to change and we find the instructions and strength to do it. Little by little, as we continue to pray and stay in God's Word, He changes us and makes us more and more like Him.

Once God begins to change us as we trust Him to do so, we can be sure He will finish the work. Philippians 1:6 says, "And I am convinced and sure of this very thing, that He Who began a good work in you will continue until the day of Jesus Christ [right up to the time of His return], developing [that good work] and perfecting and bringing it to full completion in you."

There's a Price to Pay

So, since Christ suffered in the flesh for us, for you, arm yourselves with the same thought and purpose [patiently to suffer rather than fail to please God]. For whoever has suffered in the flesh [having the mind of Christ] is done with [intentional] sin [has stopped pleasing himself and the world, and pleases God], so that he can no longer spend the rest of his natural life living by [his] human appetites and desires, but [he lives] for what God wills.

1 Peter 4:1–2

Sacrifice and *suffering* are not always popular words among Christians, but they are biblical words and words Jesus used frequently. Jesus paid the full price for all of our sins, and thankfully we never have to pay for them. But when we consider spiritual maturity or Christlikeness, it does often require us saying "no" to our selfish desires and "yes" to God. The Word of God refers to it as "dying to self." I like to say we need to "die to really live."

God's will always leads to deep joy and satisfaction, but realizing that often takes some time and experience. We have to come to the end of our own stubbornness and willful ways. When we start fully trusting God and allowing God-inspired changes in our lives, we may feel discomfort in the flesh. In other words, the flesh has a mind of its own and it does not want to give up its desires and plans. It does not want to sacrifice, to be uncomfortable or inconvenienced, or even to wait.

First Peter 4:1–2 says we can have the mind of Christ, Who suffered for us. This means we must think, *I would rather suffer and be in the will of God than suffer outside the will of God.* When we are willing to give up our own independence and submit to God, to have His will in our lives, that leads to a glorious victory, it leads to real life, the way God wants us to live it! The suffering that leads us to that good life eventually fades away and is replaced with rest, relaxation, and

amazing peace and joy. But if we stay outside God's will, we endure a miserable kind
of suffering that does not go away or lead to
breakthrough.

When I speak of suffering, I am not referring to poverty, disease, and disaster. I am
speaking of the suffering the flesh endures
when it does not get its way. The flesh is com-
posed of the soul (mind, will, and emotions)
and the body, our physical being, which has
its own desires and appetites. Even though
we have a soul and we live in a body, we are
first and foremost spiritual beings, and God
calls us to walk in the Spirit (see Galatians
5:16). This simply means we are to follow
the guidance of the Holy Spirit, Who dwells
in every believer. The Holy Spirit is to be
our guide, and He will always lead us into
truth (see John 16:13) and into God's perfect will.

For example, if Dave and I have had an
argument and I feel tension and strife between
us, I may sense the Holy Spirit urging me to
take the initiative to make peace. I may not
want to be the one to apologize first, so if

I stubbornly refuse to follow the Holy Spirit, I will suffer with the misery of knowing I was disobedient, and I will remain angry, which also makes me miserable. However, if I swallow my pride, although it is painful to do so, and do as the Holy Spirit is directing, then that momentary suffering in the flesh leads me to joy and peace.

I encourage you to be willing to pay the price for God's will in your life. The prize is well worth it!

CHAPTER 6

Worshipping Inwardly and Outwardly

For it is written, As I live, says the Lord, every knee shall bow to Me, and every tongue shall confess to God [acknowledge Him to His honor and to His praise].

Romans 14:11

We not only need to have right attitudes and worship God in our hearts, but also need to express our worship outwardly. We can demonstrate with our actions the worship and reverence we have for God in our hearts in a variety of ways. I believe one of those ways is to take Communion, which some groups call "The Lord's Supper" and some call "The Eucharist." First Corinthians 11:26 says, "For every time you eat this bread and drink this cup, you are representing and signifying and proclaiming the fact of the Lord's death until He comes [again]."

Showing with our actions what we believe in our hearts is so important. When we take Communion, we are declaring our faith with our actions, not just with what we say we believe in our hearts. Faith is powerful, but so are our actions!

When I take Communion, I say, "Lord Jesus, as I take this bread, I am taking You as my Living Bread. As long as I eat of You and fellowship with You, I will never be dissatisfied. As I take this drink, I am drinking Living Water. As long as I drink of You and fellowship with You, I will be satisfied to the point that I am not disturbed, no matter what my outward circumstances may be. I am declaring as I take Communion, Lord Jesus, that You are all I need in life to be happy and fulfilled. Thank You, Jesus, that I am forgiven for all my sins." This is also a good time to trust God for any healing you need in any area of your body.

Then I go on to say, "There are many other things I would love to have and enjoy. I can live without them if I have to, but I cannot live without You. You are my number one need."

Declare It with Actions

O clap your hands, all you peoples! Shout to God with the voice of triumph and songs of joy!

Psalm 47:1

The Bible instructs us to dance, play musical instruments, and do all kinds of things to express worship to the Lord. We need to express our worship; it brings a release in our lives; it honors God and it helps us fight and win the battles we face in life.

People have different temperaments and personalities, and there are various ways we can express our worship to God. You may prefer to worship with quiet reverence, and it's good for us to have times of stillness and quiet as we wait in God's presence. But it is also good for us to express our emotions in worship.

In some churches the congregation sings hymns and are more reserved in their worship. In other churches, people prefer outward expressions such as clapping, dancing or lifting their hands as they worship God in song.

It is beautiful to be still and quiet in God's presence, but it is equally beautiful to express sincere worship through various emotions. Our emotions are just as much a part of us as our bodies, minds, and spirits. God gave us emotions, and we need to be free to express them in worship. Emotions shouldn't control us, because they are fickle and untrustworthy, but it isn't healthy to stifle or repress them either. In Christ, we are free to express ourselves and our love for God in a balanced way.

The expressions of worship I have suggested are all biblical. You can read about them especially in the Book of Psalms. King David shouted, danced, and showed many emotions as he worshipped God. I encourage you to express your heart in your praise and worship to God. I also encourage you to pray for yourself and others, that all believers will worship God as He truly deserves to be worshipped. And finally, let me say that we should *never* criticize anyone merely because they don't do it the way we do.

Declare It with Words

Through Him, therefore, let us constantly and at all times offer up to God a sacrifice of praise, which is the fruit of lips that thankfully acknowledge and confess and glorify His name.

Hebrews 13:15

The confession of our mouths is a powerful weapon against the enemy. Proverbs 18:21 teaches that the power of life and death is in the tongue. We can speak life to ourselves and death to the enemy's plans of defeat and destruction. For example, words of thanksgiving are devastating to the enemy; he absolutely hates to hear a thankful person talking about the goodness of God.

Hebrews 4:12 teaches us that the Word of

God is a sharp, two-edged sword. I believe one edge of that sword defeats Satan, while the other releases the blessings of Heaven. Ephesians 6:17 teaches us that the "sword that the Spirit wields" (the Word of God) is part of the armor we need to effectively wage spiritual warfare.

In the Psalms, David frequently makes statements such as, "I will say of the Lord, He is my Refuge and my Fortress, my God; on Him I lean and rely, and in Him I [confidently] trust!" (Psalm 91:2). Perhaps we should regularly ask ourselves, "What am I saying about the Lord?" We need to *say* right things, not just think them. A person may think, *I believe good things about the Lord,* but it's important to also say those things. People often claim to believe something, yet everything they say indicates they believe the opposite! Words have power, so when we have right beliefs about God, we need to be sure to speak them. If you would like some specific direction and examples of how to do this, my book *The Secret Power of Speaking God's Word* would be an excellent resource.

We need to be verbal about our praise and worship toward God, and to do it at the proper times and in the proper places. I encourage you to let spoken confessions become part of your fellowship time with God. I often take walks in the morning, and as I walk, I pray, sing, or perhaps I should say I make a joyful noise that only I call singing, and confess God's Word aloud. Each time I say something like, "God is on my side. I can do whatever He assigns me to do," or "God is good and He has a good plan for my life. His blessings are overflowing toward me," it is like jabbing the enemy with a sharp sword.

Verbalize your thanksgiving, your praise, and your worship. Sing aloud songs that are filled with good things about God. This will strengthen your heart, encourage you, and help you win life's battles.

Lift Up Your Hands

O God, You are my God, earnestly will I seek You; my inner self thirsts for You, my flesh longs and is faint for You, in a dry

and weary land where no water is. So I
have looked upon You in the sanctuary to
see Your power and Your glory. Because
Your loving-kindness is better than life,
my lips shall praise You. So will I bless
You while I live; I will lift up my hands
in Your name.

Psalm 63:1–4

Sacrifice has always been a part of Christianity. From the very beginning, Old Testament law required sacrifices of various kinds. In Psalm 141:2, David speaks of the lifting of our hands "as the evening sacrifice."

Several other Scriptures also refer to the lifting of our hands (see Psalm 63:4; 134:2; 1 Timothy 2:8). This seems to be a natural thing to do when we are in the presence of God. To me, it is an expression of adoration, reverence, and surrender. We should continually surrender ourselves to God and to His plan for our lives. When we surrender, God takes control. He will not force His will on us. He waits to know that we have placed our trust in Him.

You can lift your hands and speak words of praise to God throughout the day. Even at work, you can use the privacy of a restroom break to take a moment to thank and praise God.

People who have never in their lives lifted their hands in worship to God often say they experience a tremendous release of emotions when they begin to do so. Our spirits long to worship expressively; something is missing for us spiritually until we begin to do so. I was a Christian for many years before I ever did it. I was longing for a release in praise and worship, but I had not been taught how to experience it. If something inside you is longing for that release, I encourage you to begin to worship with uplifted hands. You'll be amazed what this kind of expression of surrender and worship can do in your life.

Take a Praise Pause

Seven times a day and all day long do I praise You because of Your righteous decrees.

Psalm 119:164

I think it must bless God so much when we stop sometimes right in the middle of what we're doing and begin to praise Him. In Psalm 119:164, the psalmist said he worshipped Him *seven* times a day!

Think about a businessman, for example, maybe the CEO of a company. Wouldn't it be wonderful if, two or three times a day, he closed and locked his office door, knelt, and lifted his hands and said, "God, I just want to take some time to worship You. I appreciate all the things You do for me—the business and the success are great—but I just want to worship *You*. I magnify *You*. *You* are so wonderful. I love *You* for Who *You* are, and not merely for what You do for me!"

I believe if that businessman worshipped God in the kind of way I have described, he would not ever need to be concerned about his business, his finances, or his success. All those things would be taken care of. Matthew 6:33 says, "But seek first the kingdom of God and His righteousness, and all these things shall be added to you" (NKJV).

Just like the CEO, a stay-at-home mom would have many more peaceful, fruitful days if she took time to stop and praise and worship God. The same is true for anyone, no matter how he or she spends each day. There is no one who would not benefit from taking a "praise pause."

In addition to stopping to worship God simply to honor Him, taking time out to be in His presence is also extremely beneficial anytime we feel stressed, tired, frustrated, or tempted to give up. It will refresh us and refocus us on God. It will also make a way for Him to work on our behalf because it expresses our total trust and dependence on Him.

Bow Down

Now when Daniel knew that the writing was signed, he went into his house, and his windows being open in his chamber toward Jerusalem, he got down upon his knees three times a day and prayed and gave thanks before his God, as he had done previously.

Daniel 6:10

When we bow down, we are humbling ourselves before God. We are saying with our actions, "Lord, I worship and honor You. You are everything, and I am nothing without You."

In Daniel 6, the young man Daniel had a high position in the kingdom, and for that reason, his enemies were jealous of him. Because Daniel was a righteous man, they knew there was no way they could honestly accuse him of any wrongdoing. So they tried to find a way to weaken his devotion to God through fear of being harmed. They persuaded the king to issue a decree stating that, for thirty days, anyone caught petitioning any god or man except the king would be thrown into a den of hungry lions.

Daniel's enemies knew he had a habit of going into his room three times a day, opening his windows, and kneeling down to pray and worship God. Daniel refused to compromise his worship. After the king issued his decree, the next time Daniel knelt to worship, his enemies caught him and took him before the king, who had no choice but to throw him in the lions' den.

One of my favorite parts of this story is that Daniel prayed with his windows open, as was his custom, even when he knew that doing so would violate the decree and put his life in danger. In other words, he did not try to keep his prayer and worship a secret. He did not try to hide his faith. He had a reverential fear and awe of God that was greater than any fear of man.

Daniel did have to go into the lions' den because of his dedication to God, but he emerged unharmed the next day because God kept the lions' mouths shut. Instead of Daniel's being devoured by the lions, his enemies were thrown into the den with them and destroyed.

If you and I worship God when we have problems of any kind, we, like Daniel, will have the courage to remain faithful to Him. We may go through difficulty, but it will all work out well in the end. If we bow down on a regular basis to worship and adore Him, He will bring us through to a place of victory.

Victory is not the absence of problems; it is having peace and joy in the midst of them. Victory is continuing to bear good fruit for the kingdom of God, even when we are going through difficulties.

If we continue to worship and honor God, then no matter what the enemy brings against us, we will demonstrate our belief that God is working on our behalf and that we are confident He will bring us through our challenges victoriously. When we regularly put God first, when we worship Him and take time to bow down before Him, He will help us and lift us up.

CHAPTER 7

Worship and Prayer

While He was talking this way to them, behold, a ruler entered and, kneeling down, worshiped Him, saying, My daughter has just now died; but come and lay Your hand on her, and she will come to life.

Matthew 9:18

When Jesus went to the ruler's house and touched his daughter, she came back to life. But notice the first thing the ruler did in Matthew 9:18—not the last thing, but the first. He did not wait until he saw the manifestation of the miracle he wanted and then bow down and worship Jesus. He worshipped Him before he ever asked Him to do anything.

How many times have we asked God to

change our family members or friends without taking time to worship Him first? We say things like, "God, You've got to change my family. I just can't stand it any longer if You don't. You have got to change them, or I don't know how much longer I can hold on!"

What would happen if we changed the way we approach God about these people and the way we pray about these situations? What would happen if we just bowed down and worshipped Him, giving Him thanks, honor, and praise? What if we even went a step further and put our faces to the ground as Jehoshaphat did while waiting for God to give him victory over his enemies?

Instead of telling God how difficult our situations are and how much we need them to change, we need to say things to Him such as, "Oh, God, I worship You. I magnify Your name, Lord. You are worthy to be praised. You strengthen me when I am weak. You enable me to do what I could never do without You. I know, O God, that You have my best interests in Your heart. You are good, Father, and I believe I will see and experience

Your goodness in my life. I believe that right now You are working in my life and in my circumstances. I believe You are changing me and changing my family and friends. I believe You are dealing with those who are not born again. I believe they will accept You, be filled with Your Holy Spirit, and demonstrate Your character in their lives. I worship You, God, for the work You are doing right now and for Your faithfulness."

What do you think would begin to happen in your life if you prayed this way? I believe you would start seeing changes in your life and in your circumstances, as well as changes that need to take place in the people you love. One of the principles we see throughout Scripture, a truth that is woven through this book, is that change comes *after* we worship God, not before.

More Than a Method

I am not trying to come up with a new set of rules and regulations for answered prayer. God sees our hearts, and sincerity of heart is the most important aspect of our prayers to Him. Worshipping God before we make our requests is not a formula or a method that will work like some magic charm to help us get what we want or need. Unless our worship is real and comes out of hearts of genuine thanksgiving and praise, we may as well forget having any good results. Just because we get up in the morning and fall on our knees in praise and worship does not mean everything in our lives will change the way we want it to. Just bowing down or lifting up our hands does not mean we will receive whatever we ask for in prayer. Praising and worshipping God before asking Him for anything is not a formula to get what we want from Him. If it is taken and applied that way, it will have no power at all.

A right heart attitude—one that is sincere and genuinely loves God and wants His will—is the basis for power. God is always, first and foremost, concerned with the motives of our hearts. He always sees the "why" behind the "what." In other words,

God is not just concerned with *what* we do; He is also concerned with *why* we do it.

If we are worshipping God inwardly and outwardly because we truly believe He is worthy of praise and worship, and we believe He is the only One who can solve our problems and meet our needs, then and only then will we see positive results and experience an increase in answers to our prayers.

Prayer Changes Us

All of us want answered prayers. We would like God to simply say yes to the things we ask for. Sometimes He does say yes, and sometimes what He does for us as we pray is to change us, make us more Christlike, and empower us to minister to others more effectively.

In Luke 9, Jesus went up on a mountain to pray. Peter, James, and John were with Him. As He was praying, His appearance changed and His garments became dazzling white. Moses and Elijah conversed with Him, speaking of His exit from the Earth, which would soon come to pass.

Of course, Peter and John were astonished. They had never seen anything like this. Peter wanted to build a booth for each of them and stay on the mountain enjoying himself. Jesus, on the other hand, wanted to go back down the mountain and minister to the people.

Notice in Luke 9:29 that Jesus was changed *as He was praying*. Though the Bible does not specifically say He was worshipping, I believe Jesus always worshipped when He prayed. I certainly believe His prayers included more praise than petition. This is a lesson for all of us. If we want to see positive change in our lives, let's pray, praise, and worship. I have found that I can want to change, but after that I need to trust God to do the changing! If I merely "try," I may be somewhat successful, but it will only be behavior modification and not true heart change. As we worship, God changes our hearts. We experience His love and that causes us to respond obediently out of our love for Him.

More Praise Than Petition

When Jesus came down from the mountain, great throngs followed Him. And behold, a leper came up to Him and, prostrating himself, worshiped Him, saying, Lord, if You are willing, You are able to cleanse me by curing me. And He reached out His hand and touched him, saying, I am willing; be cleansed by being cured. And instantly his leprosy was cured and cleansed.

Matthew 8:1–3

So often, we go to God for healing, breakthrough, or deliverance, and the first thing we talk to Him about is what we need or want. We say, "Lord, I need healing. I can't stand this pain anymore. You've got to do something, Lord. You've got to change my circumstance."

But when the man in the story of Matthew 8 came to Jesus to be healed of his leprosy, he first lay facedown before Him and worshipped Him. *Then* he asked, "Lord, would You please heal me?"

This story emphasizes the lesson we learned from the story of the ruler and his daughter, at the beginning of this chapter: It is best to worship before presenting our requests. When we pray, we need more praise than petition. Asking God for things is fine. In fact, the Bible teaches us to do so (see Philippians 4:6), but I don't believe we should begin our prayers with requests. What we talk about first often reveals what is most important to us, and we need to make sure God Himself and our relationship with Him is more important to us than anything else. Remember, the Bible says we are to enter His gates with thanksgiving and come into His courts with praise (see Psalm 100:4).

If we take a close look at the prayers of the apostle Paul, we can learn some powerful lessons about what our priorities should be in our relationship with God. In Ephesians 3, he prayed above all for the people to know and experience the love of God, to have a real revelation of God's power in their lives. In

Philippians 1, he prayed for people to choose things that are excellent. In Colossians 1, he prayed that the believers would be strengthened with all power to exercise every kind of endurance and patience with joy. He also prayed many other wonderful prayers.

When I first began to closely study Paul's prayers, I realized he did not ask for material things. He was more concerned with spiritual needs than with material needs. His prayers were also filled with thanksgiving, which is a type of praise and worship.

I am sure Paul presented his physical needs to the Lord, but obviously that kind of praying did not fill much of his prayer time. We see the same principle in Jesus' prayers. He did not spend time asking for His material needs and wants to be fulfilled; He knelt in the Garden and prayed to be strengthened to do God's will (see Luke 22:41–44). When He was weary from ministering to people, He went to the mountains to pray (see Matthew 14:23; Mark 6:46), and I feel sure His prayers were filled with praise and worship.

Magnify the Lord

O magnify the Lord with me, and let us exalt His name together.

Psalm 34:3

When we pray, one thing we can do to worship God through our prayers is to magnify Him. The word *magnify* means "to enlarge." When we pray and say to the Lord, "God, I magnify You," we are saying, "I make You bigger in my life than any problem or need I have." Over the years, I have sung many songs on the theme of magnifying the Lord without even realizing what that meant. We do this a lot. We sing or talk about things we do not even understand, things that are just words or phrases we have learned in church.

We need to understand how powerful it is to magnify the Lord and make Him bigger than our problems. He truly is larger than anything in our lives, and when we worship and praise Him, we are bringing our hearts and minds into agreement with that truth.

We are saying, "You are so big and so great that all I want to do is worship You," and "You are bigger than any need I have."

When you face a battle in life, no matter how big it is, begin to pray and magnify the Lord. When He becomes bigger than your problem, you can be sure your breakthrough is on its way.

CHAPTER 8

Worship and Change

While he was still speaking, behold,
a shining cloud [composed of light]
overshadowed them, and a voice from
the cloud said, This is My Son, My
Beloved, with Whom I am [and have
always been] delighted. Listen to Him!

Matthew 17:5

Earlier in this chapter, we read that Jesus took three of His disciples up on a mountain to pray, and I said that I believe He was worshipping God as He prayed. In Matthew 17:5, we see what God said to the disciples about Jesus at that moment: "This is My beloved Son, in whom I am well pleased" (NKJV).

I believe everyone who wants to be powerful in God and victorious in life needs to hear this same message. As God's dearly loved children, we need to know He is pleased with us, personally and individually. My desire for you is that by the time you finish this book, you will know that God is pleased with you.

I express this desire realizing that you may be thinking, *Oh, no, God can't be pleased with me, not the way I act.* One of the most important things for you to know as a Christian is that God is pleased with you not because you do everything right. He is pleased with you because you put your faith in Jesus, the One who did everything right for you. Second Corinthians 5:21 says, "For our sake He made Christ [virtually] to be sin Who knew no sin, so that in and through Him we might become [endued with, viewed as being in, and examples of] the righteousness of God [what we ought to be, approved and acceptable and in right relationship with Him, by His goodness]."

God Is Changing You

Even though you have accepted what Jesus has done for you, there may still be areas of your life or ways you think or act that need to change. Because the nature of God lives in you, you can be confident that everything that needs to change will change as you trust Him.

First John 3:9 says, "No one born (begotten) of God [deliberately, knowingly, and habitually] practices sin, for God's nature abides in him [His principle of life, the divine sperm, remains permanently within him]; and he cannot practice sinning because he is born (begotten) of God."

Because you have the life of God within you, you are changing every day, and there is nothing the enemy can do about it. God is working in you, completing the good things He has begun (see Philippians 1:6).

When the enemy begins to accuse you, tries to make you feel bad about yourself, or tells you that you will never change, you can say to him, "Satan, you are a liar. I am growing spiritually and changing every day. I am getting sweeter and sweeter. I'm becoming more and more patient. I'm loving people more and more. I'm becoming more caring and more generous. I'm obeying God more quickly than I once did. I'm becoming more joyful, more peaceful, gentler, kinder, and more compassionate each day—and there is nothing you can do about it. God is in me; He is changing me! You may tell me all that is wrong with me, but I will tell you all that is right with me because of Jesus Christ!"

In the midst of the enemy's accusations, you can gain strength and victory by saying to God, "Thank You, Lord, that You are changing me. I worship You. I magnify Your name. There is none like You. I love You, Lord. I love You; I love You; I love You." This will keep your mind focused on what God is doing in your life and keep your heart open to ways He is changing you.

What Must We Do to Please God?

You and I can be confident that God is
pleased with us, yet He is also changing us
day by day. We are not where we need to be,
but thank God, we are not where we used to
be. The Lord looks at our progress, not just
at how far we still have to go.

In John 6:28, some people asked Jesus
basically, "What do we need to do to please
God?"

Jesus answered them, "Believe."

When Jesus said they needed to believe in
order to please God, He meant they needed
to believe what the Scriptures say about Him.
Let me remind you of several things God's
Word says about Jesus, truths we need to
believe. It says that Jesus, Who knew no sin,
became sin for us so we could become the
righteousness of God in Him (see 2 Corinthians 5:21). It also says that as we continue
looking into His Word, He is changing us all
the time, helping us move from one degree
of glory to the next (see 2 Corinthians 3:18).
And Deuteronomy 7:22 tells us He defeats

our enemies little by little. We can see from 2 Corinthians 3:18 and Deuteronomy 7:22 that change is a process; it takes time.

Transformation and Transfiguration

Do not be conformed to this world (this age), [fashioned after and adapted to its external, superficial customs], but be transformed (changed)…

Romans 12:2

The English word *transformation* comes from the Greek word *metamorphoo,* which means "to change into another form."[1] From *metamorphoo,* we get the English word *metamorphosis.*

The natural world gives us a great example of metamorphosis in the processes by which caterpillars become butterflies. A caterpillar eats until it grows to a certain size, and then

---

1. Definition based on W. E. Vine's *Complete Expository Dictionary of Old and New Testament Words* (Nashville: Thomas Nelson, Inc., 1984), p. 639, s.v. "transfigure," "transform."

it spins a covering, called a cocoon, around itself. It may then burrow into the ground or behind a loose piece of bark. In a way, this is like a burial.

The idea of burial is common in Scripture, both literally and symbolically. The Bible teaches us we must die to ourselves in order to live wholly for Christ. The apostle Paul writes in Galatians 2:20, "I have been crucified with Christ [in Him I have shared His crucifixion]; it is no longer I who live, but Christ (the Messiah) lives in me; and the life I now live in the body I live by faith in (by adherence to and reliance on and complete trust in) the Son of God, Who loved me and gave Himself up for me."

I have experienced this dying to self, and I still do when God is dealing with me about something I want that is not His will for me. There are things we all must die to spiritually: attitudes, thought patterns, ways of acting and speaking, our own plans and desires, and other things. This is much easier to talk about than to actually do, but we can ask

God for His grace (power, undeserved favor), and that brings about the transformation God wants in our lives.

We must go through changes that require a type of death, just as the caterpillar must go through its "burial" to be transformed into a butterfly. Dying to self is often a very personal, painful process. We cannot talk about it with just anyone. Many times, as we go through it, God assigns to us a period that I call "silent years." This is a season in which God calls us to step away from things we may have done in the past and draws us into a more hidden place so He can do a deep work in us, changing us into His image so we can live for His glory.

The Silent Years

Most people God uses endure silent years. Those are years when you are alone with your dreams for the future, and it seems as if nothing at all is happening. You are just waiting and trying not to give up! It may even seem that what is happening to you is leading you in an opposite direction than what you had imagined. This was true for Moses, Abraham, Joseph, and John the Baptist. Even Jesus had a period of time when there is no biblical record of Him other than the fact that "He grew." But the silent years are not limited to people who lived during Bible times. They still happen to people today, and as God prepares to use you in greater and greater ways, don't be surprised if you go through them too. I certainly did. Even though nothing is happening in our circumstances, a great deal is taking place in us. Like Jesus, we are growing in wisdom, experience, and knowledge of God's Word.

As God prepared me for the ministry I have today, He had to deal with me in many ways. The process took much longer than I'd expected and was more painful at times than I ever thought I could endure. Had I known ahead of time what I would have to go through in order to answer His call to ministry, I might not have said yes! I suppose this is the reason God hides certain things from us and gives us grace for them as we go through them one by one. I strongly encourage you to hold on during those silent years, and I promise that God has a right timing in your life for breakthrough!

While I was being prepared for ministry, I can assure you I did not always behave well. I had a *big* dream and a *big* vision from God, but for years, nothing *big* seemed to happen for me. I had *little* opportunities, but since I had a *big* vision, I did not appreciate the small things God allowed me to do. Much of the time, I was frustrated and unthankful for the things I was able to do.

I was not always a woman of faith. I experienced many emotional ups and downs and lots of anger when things did not go my way. I had great difficulty submitting to authority and did not display much of the fruit of the Spirit. As a believer, I had the seeds of those fruits in me, but it took time for them to develop.

To fulfill God's call on my life, I needed to be changed. I still do, but at least I understand the process now. I have compassion for people who fight God for years, not understanding what He is really trying to do in their lives. We should trust Him in the hard times. We should worship in the wilderness, not just in the Promised Land. Remember, the Israelites worshipped God after they crossed the Red Sea and were safe. They sang the right song on the wrong side of the Red Sea. God wants to hear our praise *before* we experience victory. That's one way we win the battles of life.

I went through years when the enemy told me over and over that I was crazy, that God had not really called me into ministry and that I would never change, and I would fail. He assured me that nothing I did would bear good fruit and that my suffering would never end. He told me I was a fool for believing something I could not see.

God gave me the grace to press on, little by little. I changed by the grace of God, and things in my life changed in corresponding ways. We need to know that God releases to us the things we can handle properly, and thankfully does not give us what we cannot handle well and with humility. The worst condition a person can be in is to have something he or she is not prepared to handle. God knows what we can manage and steward well. He will release those things when we are ready for them, rather than simply giving us what we ask for when He knows those things would become burdens or problems for us.

God has changed me so much over the years that sometimes I can barely remember how I used to be. My silent years were difficult, but when they were over, I was thankful for the work God had done in me by His grace. I didn't like or understand those years while they were taking place, but I would not be who I am or where I am today without them.

If you have a dream or vision for God to use you, be prepared to endure some silent years. Keep a heart of worship throughout that time, knowing God is changing you for His glory, and one day, you will look back and be thankful for all He has done in your life. When you start to feel weary, declare loudly,

"God is changing me. He is preparing me for good things."

The Rest of God

So then, there is still awaiting a full and complete Sabbath-rest reserved for the [true] people of God; for he who has once entered [God's] rest also has ceased from [the weariness and pain] of human labors, just as God rested from those labors peculiarly His own.

Hebrews 4:9–10

When I began to study the process of metamorphosis and realized how it applied to our spiritual lives, I saw that the time a cocoon spends burrowed into the ground or behind a piece of bark is a time of rest. The cocoon doesn't really do anything; it simply allows change to happen. The caterpillar is gradually transformed into a butterfly and emerges from its cocoon as a brand-new creature.

If you are troubled or upset by the changes that need to happen in you, I have good news: You can enter the rest of God. You can relax and let God do the work. Struggling, frustration, and worry will not change you. The more you rest in God, the faster you will see change. God knows what He is doing in you and He knows how to do it. If you stop fighting and surrender to His work, you will be more at peace, and He will do what He needs to do in you. Simply say, "Lord, I can't change myself. I believe You are the only One Who can do the work that needs to be done in me. I place myself entirely in Your hands, and I wait on You to make the changes You know need to be made in me. I trust Your ways and I trust Your timing." This way, you can enjoy fellowship with God without being uptight about what's happening in your life. You can relax and let Him do what He needs to do.

The process of transformation will probably be painful at times. Let it hurt. The more you fight it, the longer it takes. A pregnant woman giving birth is always told to relax and breathe. If you relax through the painful times in your life, God will keep moving you closer to your breakthrough. Above all, trust God and love Him with your whole heart. Worship Him, praise Him, and be very thankful!

I encourage you to tell the Lord, "When You are finished with this part of my transformation process, I don't even want to recognize myself. I am a new creature in Christ, and I want to behave like one. I want to be more like Jesus!"

Worship Instead of Worry

Sometimes, when we are going through difficult times, we have a hard time seeing anything good in our lives. This is because we are looking at the wrong things and worrying about them. We look too much at what is wrong with us and not enough at what is right with Jesus. Hebrews 12:2 tells us to look to Him because He is the Source and the Finisher of our faith.

In Numbers 21, many Israelites were dying in the wilderness because a plague of snakes had been released among them as a result of their sin. In the midst of this, Moses prayed and worshipped God. He turned his attention immediately to God, not to himself or to anyone else, to solve the problem. In fact, throughout the Bible, when people had problems, the ones who ended up victorious refused to worry. They worshipped.

Moses sought God about how to handle the snakes. He did not make his own plan and ask God to bless it; he did not try to reason out an answer with his own mind, nor did he worry. He worshipped God, and that brought an answer from God. We see that answer in Numbers 21:8: "And the Lord said to Moses, Make a fiery serpent [of bronze] and set it on a pole; and everyone who is bitten, when he looks at it, shall live." Frustrated people usually don't hear from God, but when we enter His rest through worship, His direction becomes clear.

The pole with the bronze serpent represented the cross, where Jesus paid for our

sin. The same message God gave the Israelites applies to us today: "Look and live." If
we look to Jesus and worship Him instead
of worrying, God will bring us victory in the
battles we face in our lives.

CHAPTER 9

Worship God with a Pure Conscience

I thank God Whom I worship with a pure conscience, in the spirit of my fathers, when without ceasing I remember you night and day in my prayers.

2 Timothy 1:3

True worship must come from the heart of a worshiper. It is not, and can never be, merely a learned behavior. God is interested in people's hearts above all else. He is looking for people who have sincere hearts that truly love Him and genuinely desire to worship Him. On the other hand, if the heart is not pure, nothing that comes from a person is acceptable. Works offered with impure motives are not acceptable; the same is true for feigned acts of worship that do not come from pure hearts and clean consciences.

The conscience can be a person's best friend because it continually and unrelentingly helps a believer know what is pleasing to God and what is not. It is the best preacher anyone can ever have in his or her life, and it is designed to teach us and lead us into God's will. God's Word enlightens the conscience; therefore, the more of His Word a person learns, the more active his or her conscience will be.

An Enlightened Conscience

I am speaking the truth in Christ. I am not lying; my conscience [enlightened and prompted] by the Holy Spirit bearing witness with me.

Romans 9:1

Paul refers to his conscience being enlightened by the Holy Spirit. His conscience told him whether or not his behavior was acceptable to God, and I am sure he could also discern through his conscience when his thoughts, words, or actions were not acceptable. This is the function of the conscience.

In Acts 24:16, Paul writes of the importance of keeping the conscience clean: "Therefore I always exercise and discipline myself [mortifying my body, deadening my carnal affections, bodily appetites, and worldly desires, endeavoring in all respects] to have a clear (unshaken, blameless) conscience, void of offense toward God and toward men."

Since Paul made such an effort to have a clear conscience, surely it must be very important. We know from 2 Timothy 1:3 that Paul worshipped God with a pure conscience, and that is the same way we need to worship God. Worshipping from a clear, clean conscience is the only way we can offer Him acceptable worship.

I do not want to use worship as a means of obtaining blessings or breakthroughs from the Lord. He definitely does bring victory in the lives of those who worship, but true worship comes only from a pure heart and a clean conscience.

Simply stated, this means we cannot properly worship God with known sin in our lives. The repentance of sin should be the prelude to real worship because we must approach God with a clean conscience. The person who has a guilty conscience will not experience peace. His or her faith will not work, nor will their prayers be answered (see 1 Timothy 1:19; 3:9).

Be Perfect

You, therefore, must be perfect [growing into complete maturity of godliness in mind and character, having reached the proper height of virtue and integrity], as your heavenly Father is perfect.

Matthew 5:48

The Bible commands us to be perfect even as our Father in Heaven is perfect. Unless we understand this instruction correctly, we immediately feel defeated and even fearful when we read it. The Amplified translation, quoted above, makes it clear that "perfect" is a state of spiritual maturity we grow into. We must continue pressing toward the mark of perfection out of a sincere heart that wants to please God, daily letting go of mistakes that lie behind us.

In other words, our hearts can be perfect through being born again, but our behavior is not. We improve all the time, and we thank God for that, but we have not arrived. We are perfected in Christ, but in and of ourselves, we are still growing toward perfection through the grace of God working daily in our lives.

The Pathway to a Clear Conscience

To have a clear conscience, people must either not sin or repent of their sins when they do make mistakes. We do grow and find that we sin less and less as time goes by; however, the Bible teaches us that a little leaven affects the whole lump of dough. Even a little sin puts us in need of cleansing.

Making progress daily is great, but I am very thankful for the gift of repentance. First

John 1:9 promises that we can admit our sins and confess them, and that God is faithful to completely cleanse us of all unrighteousness. What good news! We can live before God with a perfectly clear conscience, because there is no condemnation to those in Christ (see Romans 8:1).

The reason Paul lived before God or other people with a perfectly clear conscience was not that he never made mistakes. In fact, the opposite is true. He did make mistakes. He called himself the chief of sinners and said he had not arrived at a place of perfection (see 1 Timothy 1:15; Philippians 3:12).

Through desiring hearty obedience and using the gift of repentance when he failed, Paul lived before God and others with a clear conscience and was, therefore, enabled to worship God properly and trust God to meet his needs.

Why do I refer to repentance as a gift? I have seen people who could not feel sorry for their sins, and that is a terrible thing. When the conscience is seared (hardened), people are unable to feel the weight and seriousness of their wrong behavior. Because of this, we should pray for a tender conscience toward God.

What to Do When Your Conscience Convicts You

The enemy *condemns* us; the Holy Spirit *convicts* us. Conviction is not meant to make us feel guilty or worse about something we have done; it is intended to help us feel better. For years, I did not know this truth, and when the Holy Spirit convicted me, I responded improperly by feeling guilty and condemned. It was horrible! I had become a serious student of God's Word, so the more I studied and learned how I was supposed to live, the more I felt condemned when I was not living that way. I seemed to feel guilty and condemned about something almost all the time.

When I finally saw the truth that the Holy Spirit was convicting me so He could help me break free from sin, I felt a wonderful release. Now I am glad when I feel convicted. I'm not glad I am sinning, but I am glad I can repent and ask God to forgive me and help me grow beyond it. I can also now discern when the enemy is coming against me to make me feel guilty and I resist him.

I really want to encourage you not to do things you do not have peace about doing. Let your conscience be your friend, not a source of torment. Colossians 3:15 says that peace is like an umpire in our lives; it should settle with finality all the things that raise questions in our minds. In other words, if you feel peace about something, it can stay in your life. If you don't feel peace about it, throw it out.

Being tempted by sin is not the same as sinning. Temptation is not sin. We are all tempted to do wrong; Satan makes sure of that. When we are tempted, though, we can call on the Holy Spirit to help us resist. We don't need to try to resist in our own strength and power; we simply need to ask for the Holy Spirit's help. He is always standing by to help us with anything we need in life.

Thank God for Forgiveness

Following the leading of the Holy Spirit and therefore obeying God is always our best course of action, but the fact is: We all make mistakes. None of us is one hundred percent obedient all the time. There are times when even the most dedicated, sincere Christians make wrong choices. That's when we need to quickly repent, ask for God's forgiveness, and receive it.

We would be wise to begin our prayers with repentance to clear our consciences of any sin we have committed, knowingly or unknowingly. Our forgiveness has already been paid for by the death and resurrection of Jesus, and all we need to do is ask and receive that our joy may be full (see John 16:24). If we are aware of any certain situations or if He brings anything to mind, we can repent specifically. King David even asked God to forgive him for unconscious and hidden faults. He wanted to come into God's presence totally free and ready to pray boldly. We can ask the Lord to convict us of sin and tell Him we want to change and do things right. We can then ask Him for His grace, which is His enabling power to help us not make the same mistakes in the future. If we do these things not as a ritual or a method, but with pure hearts, we will be able to worship with clear consciences.

CHAPTER 10

God Is for You

What then shall we say to [all] this? If God is for us, who [can be] against us? [Who can be our foe, if God is on our side?]

Romans 8:31

God is a big God; nothing is impossible with Him, and He is on our side. We have nothing to fear from our enemies because none of them is as great or powerful as our God. God is for us. The enemy is against us; that's his only position. But God is over us, under us, and through us. He goes before us and behind us, and He surrounds us.

Psalm 125:1–2 says: "Those who trust in, lean on, and confidently hope in the Lord are like Mount Zion, which cannot be moved but abides and stands fast forever. As the mountains are round about Jerusalem, so the Lord is round about His people from this time forth and forever."

Like Mount Zion, we should not be moved by the storms of life, because God is all around us. And if that is not enough, He is also in us and will never leave us or forsake us (see 1 Corinthians 3:16; Deuteronomy 31:6). Since these things are true, we are ready for any battle, and we have no reason to feel threatened or intimidated by the enemy or by other people. We are completely safe and we have nothing to fear.

Fear the Lord, Not People

Let those now who reverently and worshipfully fear the Lord say that His mercy and loving-kindness endure forever. Out of my distress I called upon the Lord; the Lord answered me and set me free and in a large place. The Lord is on my side; I will not fear. What can man do to me?

Psalm 118:4–6

In the first verse of this passage, the psalmist is worshipping God for some of His attributes, specifically His mercy and loving-kindness. Meditating on God's attributes and praising Him for them builds our faith in Him.

In the second verse, notice that the psalmist did not call on the Lord in his distress until after he first praised and worshipped God for the very things he needed in his time of trouble.

In the third verse, the psalmist declares: "The Lord is on my side; I will not fear." Why should we fear? If Almighty God is for us, and He is, then what can mere human beings do to us? We need to realize how big God is and how small our enemies are.

Even though we have no reason to fear others, some people spend a lot of time worrying or being afraid of what someone else might do to them. You may even be worried about what people may do to you. You may be concerned that someone will take your job or that you will lose an important relationship or that you will not have what you need. Or perhaps you are afraid of what someone will think of you or say about you.

The Bible tells us in Psalm 118:4 that we are not to fear people, but we are to reverently and worshipfully fear the Lord. Proverbs 29:25 is very clear about this: "The fear of man brings a snare, but whoever leans on, trusts in, and puts his confidence in the Lord is safe and set on high." When we refuse to be afraid of other people, but reverently fear the Lord and trust Him instead, He moves on our behalf so that nothing anyone tries to do ever permanently harms us. People may come against us one way, but they have to flee from us in many directions. Deuteronomy 28:7 says: "The Lord shall cause your enemies who rise up against you to be defeated before your face; they shall come out against you one way and flee before you seven ways."

For a period of time, someone may seem to be taking advantage of us or coming against us. But if we keep our eyes on God and continue to worship Him, desiring His will in all things, in the end God will reward us and bring justice to our situations because He is a God of justice and hates wrongdoing (see Isaiah 61:8).

We prolong our troubles when we try to make people give us what we think is due us. Instead of doing that, we should wait on the Lord, and let Him bring us what we are supposed to have. God is our Vindicator. We cannot vindicate ourselves, and we actually make matters worse when we try.

We need to retire from caring so much about what others think or what they may try to do to us. Instead, we should cast our care upon the Lord because He cares for us (see 1 Peter 5:7). If our hearts are focused on Him, no one will take advantage of us for very long or hurt us in permanent ways. God has thousands of ways to get His blessings to us and to protect us from evil or harm. This is why our attitude should be, "If God is for us, who [can be] against us?" (Romans 8:31).

What Can People Do?

God's Word is filled with promises that He will take care of us. One of those promises is stated so beautifully that I don't see how we could read it and remain fearful.

...For He [God] Himself has said, I will not in any way fail you nor give you up nor leave you without support. [I will] not, [I will] not, [I will] not in any degree leave you helpless nor forsake nor let [you] down (relax My hold on you)! [Assuredly not!] So we take comfort and are encouraged and confidently and boldly say, The Lord is my Helper; I will not be seized with alarm [I will not fear or dread or be terrified]. What can man do to me?

Hebrews 13:5–6

These verses are very comforting to me. They are emphatic, stating *three times* that God will not leave us helpless. I encourage you to meditate on these Scriptures anytime fear comes against your mind for any reason. The Word of God has inherent power, and simply meditating on it will help you feel better.

Reverent Fear of God

But as for me, I will enter Your house through the abundance of Your steadfast love and mercy; I will worship toward and at Your holy temple in reverent fear and awe of You.

Psalm 5:7

When we talk about fearing God, we are not talking about the wrong kind of fear. We are talking about a reverential fear that causes us to be in awe of Him, bow in His presence, and even prostrate ourselves before Him and say, "My God, there is none like You. Whom shall I fear? If You are for me, what can any human being do against me?"

The apostle Paul said in Galatians 1:10, "Now am I trying to win the favor of men, or of God? Do I seek to please men? If I were still seeking popularity with men, I should not be a bond servant of Christ (the Messiah)." This Scripture has always gripped my heart because I know how rejection from other people has tried to prevent me from moving forward in God's call on my life.

We have all been attacked by rejection, which is one way the enemy keeps us from going forward. He knows we will be blessed as we do God's will, so he uses the fear that people will reject us to hold us back.

The enemy has launched attacks of rejection against me during many important seasons in my life and in my walk with God. Many times, those attacks came through people I loved and cared about, and that was especially painful. Sometimes, in order to please people, I wanted to give in to the pressure and stop pursuing the things of God so passionately. I shudder to think what would have happened to me had I done that. I'm sure I would not be where I am today. I can look back and see that every time an attack of rejection came against me, it happened when God was trying to do something new in me or take me to the next level of what He had for my life.

People who want to do God's will must fear God more than they fear other people.

We all want to be accepted, and rejection is always painful, but if we reverently fear the Lord and determine to follow Him instead of trying to please others, He will bless us. No matter what others may try to do to you, God is your Vindicator (see Psalm 135:14), and your reward comes from Him.

God wants you and me to resist and stand strong against the fear of other people and the fear of rejection. We may feel fear, but we don't have to bow down to its demands. God knows we will never become all He wants us to be or do everything He wants us to do if those fears control us. We need to care more about what He thinks than we care about what others think because He is our Protector (see Psalm 91:1–2), our Provider (see Philippians 4:19), our Deliverer (see Psalm 68:20), and our Victory (see 1 Corinthians 15:57).

CHAPTER 11

God Will Provide

He has given food and provision to those who reverently and worshipfully fear Him; He will remember His covenant forever and imprint it [on His mind].

Psalm 111:5

Many times, the battles we face in our lives are focused on our provision. We may be afraid we will not have what we need, or we may not be sure where our provision will come from. Over the years, I have conducted surveys among people who attend our conferences and found that at least 50 percent of the people in our audiences are fearful about some aspect of provision for their lives.

The Bible contains many stories about people who needed provision, and God came through for them in miraculous ways. We find two examples of this in the same chapter—1 Kings 17. God once directed Elijah, whom I will write about later in this book, to rest beside a brook for a while. The whole time he was there, a famine was in the land, but ravens brought him food. After he left the brook, God sent him to meet a poor widow who only had enough flour and oil to prepare a final meal for herself and her son. Elijah asked her to make him something to eat, and she did—even though she knew it would take everything she had left. After that, God provided for her in such a way that she never again ran out of flour and oil. The widow needed a miracle, and in order to have it, she needed to give, so God sent her someone she could help. Our giving in faith is one of the ways we worship God. By giving some of what we have, even though it seems that we don't have enough for ourselves, we are saying by our actions, "God, I trust You to provide."

In Psalm 111:5, the psalmist is praising and worshipping God for His great works on behalf of His people. This tells us that as long as we worship God, we will have His provision. We continually see the same theme in God's Word: Worship wins the battle.

Maybe you have been told you are going to lose your job or your housing. Maybe you are living on a retirement budget or a fixed income, and you wonder what is going to happen in the future. You see prices rising on everything, almost every time you go to a store, and the enemy whispers in your ear, "You are not going to have enough to live on." Or maybe the numbers just don't add up and your income is not enough to support you, yet you are doing everything you know to do.

Whatever the reason for your concern about your provision, take Psalm 111:5 and digest it. Meditate on it by turning it over and over in your mind, really thinking about what it means for you individually. Think about it, pray about it, and let it become real and personal to you.

This verse says God gives food and provision to those who reverently fear Him and worship Him. That means that whatever your situation may be, God will provide for you as long as you worship and magnify Him. So don't worry about provision. The battle belongs to the Lord, and He will take care of you as you continue to honor and worship Him.

Worship Is Wisdom

The reverent fear and worship of the Lord is the beginning of Wisdom...

Psalm 111:10

If you read the book of Proverbs and look at the radical promises made to the person who walks in wisdom, and then realize that worship and the reverent fear of the Lord are the beginning of wisdom, you will quickly see why worship is so important.

The Bible says those who walk in wisdom will be exceedingly happy and prosperous, and that they will live long lives (see Proverbs 3:1–8), but there is no such thing as wisdom without worship. Many people today are seeking knowledge, and knowledge is good, but wisdom is better. Wisdom is the right use of knowledge. Knowledge without wisdom can cause people to be puffed up with pride, which will ultimately ruin their lives. Wise people are knowledgeable, but not all knowledgeable people are wise.

I believe our society today exalts knowledge more than we should. Education seems to be many people's main goal, yet our world is in rapid moral decline. Education is good, but not better than wisdom. We need to seek wisdom as diligently as we would look for silver or gold and to make it a vital necessity in our lives. Wisdom is vital to a successful Christian life, and the beginning of wisdom is worship.

There Is No Want in Worship

The Angel of the Lord encamps around those who fear Him [who revere and worship Him with awe] and each of them He delivers. O taste and see that the Lord [our God] is good! Blessed (happy, fortunate, to be envied) is the man who trusts and takes refuge in Him. O fear the Lord, you His saints [revere and worship Him]! For there is no want to those who truly revere and worship Him with godly fear.

Psalm 34:7–9

Do you want angels to go to work in your life? Then start worshipping God because Psalm 34:7–9 says His Angel encamps around and watches over those who revere and worship Him.

Do you want to be sure all your needs will be met? Then worship God because His Word says there is no want, no lack, to those who truly worship and fear Him.

You may be worshipping and fearing God, yet you do not see Him moving in your life. So you may ask, "If He does these things for those who worship Him, why am I worshipping and seeing nothing?"

I believe God is moving in your life. I believe He is doing great things on your behalf. He is doing great things in all of our lives, if we would only recognize them. Often we spend our time counting up what we don't have instead of what we do have. We think about what we have lost instead of what we have left. This prevents us from realizing how truly blessed we are.

Having a thankful heart is part of worship, and it is certainly the attitude of a worshipper. God does a lot with a little, and He does the most with nothing. He uses things the world considers "nothings" and people the world considers "nobodies" to do His work through, according to 1 Corinthians 1:26–29. So even if we had nothing, we could give it to God, and He would do something with it. God has no problem providing us with whatever we need in this life. If we will only worship Him, cast our cares on Him, and obey His instructions, we will always have our needs met.

I have lost a lot in my life. I was abused during my childhood so I never really had the chance to be a child. For a long time, I really resented what I had lost. I resented the years I could never get back; and I resented not having a good start in life because I knew a lot of my problems as an adult came from the things that were wrong about my early years.

Finally, I saw I could not do anything about what I had lost, and I started looking at what I had left. For one thing, I had the rest of my life, and so do you. Even if the years you have lived have not been pleasant, you still have your future.

I began to worship God right where I was, and I trusted Him to be faithful to His Word. I gave Him what I had left. I said, "Lord, here I am. I am not much, but if You can use me, I'm Yours."

I encourage you to begin to worship God right where you are. Worship Him for what you do have, and forget about what you do not have. There is no want in worship. As we worship God, He meets all of our needs.

The Enemy Steals, God Provides

The Old Testament includes many stories about the enemies of Israel and Judah, enemies who wanted to destroy God's people.

Likewise, you and I have an enemy, Satan. He has a plan to destroy us. He is working on that plan, and part of the way he does it is to steal from us and bring loss into our lives. But God has a plan to surprise him and bring us victory. We can be confident of this, and this is why we can worship God in faith when we find ourselves in the battles of life.

A good friend who is a Greek scholar once shared with me a paraphrase of John 10:10. It gives us a clear idea of just how determined the enemy is to kill, steal, and destroy, but it also shows us that Jesus has something else altogether in mind.

The thief wants to get his hands into every good thing in your life. In fact, this pickpocket is looking for any opportunity to wiggle his way so deeply into your personal affairs that he can walk off with everything you hold precious and dear. And that's not all—when he's finished stealing all your goods and possessions, he'll take his plan to rob you blind to the next level. He'll create conditions and situations so horrible that you'll see no way to solve the problem except to sacrifice everything that remains from his previous attacks. The goal of this thief is to totally waste and devastate your life. If nothing stops him, he'll leave you insolvent, flat broke, and cleaned out in every area of your life. You'll end up feeling as if you are finished and out of business! Make no mistake—the enemy's ultimate aim is to obliterate you!

But I came that they might have, keep, and constantly retain a vitality, gusto, vigor, and zest for living that springs up from deep down inside. I came that they might embrace this unrivaled, unequaled, matchless, incomparable, richly-loaded and overflowing life to the ultimate maximum![2]

I am so glad for the words *But I have come,* spoken by Jesus Himself. He is always able

---

2. Rick Renner. *Sparkling Gems* (Tulsa, OK: Harrison House and Teach All Nations, 2003), 548.

to interrupt the enemy's plan and to bring us victory. As I said earlier, no one gets through life without battles. But those battles belong to the Lord, and if we worship Him through them, He will bring us to victory.

Praise Saves

I will call upon the Lord, Who is to be praised; so shall I be saved from my enemies.

Psalm 18:3

The psalmist said that when he needed to be saved from his enemies, he would call upon the Lord, Who is to be praised. When you and I face battles in our lives, if we get into God's presence and praise Him, our enemies will get so confused they will begin to attack each other. That is exactly what happened to Jehoshaphat's enemies and to Gideon's enemies.

When our enemies try to upset us and we respond by praising God, it confuses them so much that they begin to attack one another. And in the process, we find a new level of joy.

As we have seen, there is too much fear among God's people. But the Lord says, "Fear not [there is nothing to fear], for I am with you" (Isaiah 41:10). Under the Old Covenant, God was with His people—and look at the awesome victories He gave them. But we can go far beyond that because the same God Who led the Israelites to victory after victory over their enemies is not only *with* us, but also *in* us as born-again believers in Jesus.

I like to think God is as close to me as my next breath, and I need Him as much as I need each breath to live. God is our life. Acts 17:28 says, "In Him we live and move and have our being." God is everything, and He is worthy of our praise and worship.

CHAPTER 12

God Is on Your Side

Little children, you are of God [you belong to Him] and have [already] defeated and overcome them [the agents of the antichrist], because He Who lives in you is greater (mightier) than he who is in the world.

1 John 4:4

People have so many fears that we could spend all day naming them and probably not run out of them. Many believers have the same fears everyone else has, even though the Bible tells us many times to not be afraid. First John 4:4 is a "power verse" against fear. It assures us that because of the presence and power of Almighty God within us, we do not need to be afraid of *anything*.

When you begin to feel afraid, 1 John 4:4 is a great verse to read aloud. You can even say, "Satan, I don't have to be afraid of you because God's Word says I have already defeated you through my relationship with Jesus. God is far greater than you are, and He is on my side!"

Do you know what the Bible means when it says you and I are more than conquerors through Jesus Christ (see Romans 8:37)? I believe it means we do not have to live in fear. Before a battle even begins, we have already been told that we will win it. We know the outcome—we can enter God's rest knowing we will come through it victoriously.

We may not like having to go through our battles. Resisting fear may not be easy. But we can be encouraged, knowing that whatever the enemy means for our harm, God intends for our good (see Genesis 50:20).

If God is on our side, and if we are on His side, in the end everything is going to work out for our good because whoever is with the Lord is on the winning team.

"But God..."

But God shows and clearly proves His [own] love for us by the fact that while we were still sinners, Christ (the Messiah, the Anointed One) died for us.

Romans 5:8

There is a very short phrase in the Bible that changes everything for us. It is just two little words, but it occurs throughout the Bible and is one of the most powerful two-word phrases in all of Scripture. It is simply: "But God..."

As we go through the Bible, we constantly read disastrous reports of the terrible things the enemy had planned for God's people. Then we come to these words—*But God*—and the next thing we read about is a victory.

Romans 5:8 mentions that we are all sinners, a condition that deserves punishment and death. The phrase *But God* interrupts the process. God's love comes into a situation and changes everything. While we were sinners, Christ died for us and, by doing so, proved

His love for us. He proved that His love interrupts the devastation of sin.

Not only does God's love interrupt the devastation of our own sin, but it also interrupts the plans of the enemy. That certainly happened in the life of Joseph. When his brothers sold him into slavery, God was with him, and he ended up in a high government position (see Genesis 37:28; 41:41–43).

God's love for you can interrupt the plans of the enemy or the plans of other people against you too. For example, maybe you had a certain job for ten years and you were counting on that job for years in the future. But something happened and the company folded; your future seemed to be destroyed. *But God* can put you in a far better job than you had, perhaps one with better pay or benefits, a better work environment, or better chances for advancement and success in the future. He can even give you favor and help you get a job for which you may not even be qualified, naturally speaking, and then give you grace to do it well. He can enable you to do something no one in the world, including yourself, would have ever thought you were capable of doing.

We should learn to look at things through the eyes of faith instead of with our natural sight. What normally happens in a situation can be totally changed when God comes on the scene.

When God called me into the ministry, some friends told me, "Joyce, some of us have been talking and we feel there is no way you are ever going to be able to do what you say God has told you that you will do. We just don't feel your personality is suitable for that kind of job."

I still remember how awful I felt when they said those things to me. I was hurt and discouraged—but God had called me, and He qualified me. What others thought was not even usable, God saw value in. He helped me, and He will do the same for you. When people tell us certain things are impossible or highly unlikely—and even if we ourselves begin to doubt—we should not give up. We should worship and watch God work on our behalf. All things are possible with God to those who believe (see Mark 9:23).

"The Lord Is with Us!"

Joshua and Caleb were two men of God who found themselves involved with a group of people who were negative and full of unbelief. Joshua and Caleb would not allow these people to influence them in an adverse way; they remained full of faith and confidence that they could conquer their enemies.

Likewise, you and I must be determined not to let negative people steal our joy by taking away our positive attitudes. We cannot allow them to destroy our confidence that God is good and has a good plan for our lives. The enemy uses negative, doubt-filled people to drain our joy, so we must be diligent not to let them do so.

There are times in life when circumstances are not very exciting. We look around and see problems that seem like giants to us, but we need to remember that God is greater than the giants. Joshua and Caleb found themselves in this kind of situation. Moses sent them and ten other men into the Promised Land of Canaan to spy out the land and bring back a report describing it. Ten of the men came back and said, "The land is full of good fruit, but it is also full of giants, and we cannot defeat them."

But Joshua and Caleb had a different attitude. They had also seen the giants, but preferred to keep their eyes on God, Whom they believed to be greater than the giants. They said, "Let us go up at once and possess it; we are well able to conquer it" (Numbers 13:30). The negative people responded immediately, "We are not able" (Numbers 13:31).

This is the way things often are in life. There are always positive people who are trying to go forward, and then there are negative people who try to contaminate good things with their bad attitudes. Ten of the spies were negative and two were positive. Based on those figures, most of the people said they were not able to defeat the giants, while only two believed God's power was greater than the problem. If a larger percentage of people believed in the great power of God, we would see more people succeeding than we do.

Sad to say, we often focus our eyes on the giants, or the things that stand in our way, instead of on God. We lose our focus; we become entangled with our problems and lose sight of what God has called us to do. I believe more time spent worshipping and praising God would help us keep a clear focus and enable us to go forward with strong, positive attitudes, believing we can do anything God tells us to do. Spend more time praising God for what He has already done in your life and worshipping Him because of His greatness, and the fact that there is nothing that He cannot do.

Joshua and Caleb reminded the others that God had promised to give them the land. They encouraged them not to rebel against the Lord and not to fear the people. They said, "The Lord is with us" (Numbers 14:9).

God is not with the enemy; He is with us: "If God is for us, who [can be] against us?" (Romans 8:31). I encourage you to practice maintaining a good attitude. Be content and thankful. Notice what God *is* doing, not just what you think He is *not* doing, for you. Beware of complaining. Instead, worship God and keep worshipping Him until your breakthrough comes. Having a good attitude will bring your breakthrough more quickly than being negative. No matter how long you have to wait for your victory to come, you might as well be happy. This is called "enjoying where you are on the way to where you're going."

Regardless of our current circumstances, we know that God is with us. In fact, He is actually way ahead of us. He knows the outcome of our situation, and His plan is for our good, not for failure.

Fear Not: God Goes Before You

It is the Lord Who goes before you; He will [march] with you; He will not fail you or let you go or forsake you; [let there be no cowardice or flinching, but] fear

*not, neither become broken [in spirit—
depressed, dismayed, and unnerved with
alarm].*

Deuteronomy 31:8

In Deuteronomy 31:8, Moses told Joshua he was to be strong, courageous, and firm because he would lead the people into the land the Lord had given them. He assured Joshua that the Lord would never fail or forsake him but that He would go before him to lead him to victory. That same promise is true for you and me today.

It is comforting to think that everywhere we go, God has been before us, preparing the way. I have some understanding of what this means because when Dave and I travel, especially internationally, we send a team of people into a city to prepare the way for us before we arrive. They make sure they have directions for all the places we need to go; they check the hotels and confirm all of our arrangements so that when we arrive, we can focus on ministering to people rather than getting entangled in details we don't need to be involved in. This makes our ministry much more fruitful.

One time we had planned a conference outside the United States. When our employee arrived several months in advance of the event, he realized the arena we had planned to use was in a part of the city that would be very difficult to travel to and from. Traffic would be heavy before and after our meetings, and there was only one road in and one road out of the venue, meaning people might have spent as many as four hours in traffic to get where they needed to go. Sending an employee well ahead of the event proved to be very fruitful. He was able to change the meeting place and save us a lot of time.

Knowing someone goes ahead of us when we travel is very comforting to me, and I have confidence that everything is as it should be. Likewise, knowing God has gone before me in every situation of my life gives me comfort and confidence, and I am free to live without fear.

For example, if you have a court case coming up, you need to understand that God has gone before you into the courtroom, before you ever arrive. Or if you need to confront your employer about some issue at work, believe what the Bible says—that God will go before you and prepare the way, that He will give you favor and even give you the right words to say when the time comes. Release your faith in the God Who goes before you, and believe He has prepared your way.

I also encourage you to be careful of your thoughts when facing situations like these. We often pray and ask God for help, even for miracles, but in our thoughts and imaginations, we see disaster and failure. We need to eliminate every thought that does not agree with God's Word. The psalmist said, "Let the words of my mouth and the meditation of my heart be acceptable in Your sight, O Lord" (Psalm 19:14). God is pleased with our thoughts and words when they agree with His Word.

When we need God's power to help us in a situation, we cannot ask for something positive and then speak negatively about those circumstances. It is very important to ask for what we need and then keep our thoughts and words in line with what we have asked for according to God's Word.

CHAPTER 13

Remain in Position

Elijah was a human being with a nature such as we have [with feelings, affections, and a constitution like ours]; and he prayed earnestly for it not to rain, and no rain fell on the earth for three years and six months. And [then] he prayed again and the heavens supplied rain and the land produced its crops [as usual].

James 5:17–18

In 1 Kings 17:1, Elijah the prophet told wicked King Ahab that no rain would fall on the land of Israel for a certain amount of time, according to the word of the Lord. I'm sure it took courage for him to announce such bad news to the king, but Elijah feared

God more than man, and he was obedient to deliver the word.

During the time of drought, God took care of Elijah. First, He hid him by a brook and sent ravens to deliver food to him (see 1 Kings 17:2–6). When the brook dried up, God sent Elijah to the home of a poor widow and miraculously provided for the widow, her son, and Elijah until He sent rain on the land once again (see 1 Kings 17:7–24).

After these years, the Lord sent Elijah back to King Ahab to tell him it was about to rain again. Ahab was a very wicked man, and where there is wickedness, there will always be drought and famine of some kind. When people are not serving God, they will experience spiritual, emotional, and physical lack.

Elijah's Message to Ahab

And Elijah said to Ahab, Go up, eat and drink, for there is the sound of abundance of rain.

1 Kings 18:41

God had brought drought and famine on Israel to show His power to Ahab and to let Ahab and his wife, Jezebel, know they needed to change their wicked ways. If they did not, things would not be good.

After three years of famine, God sent His prophet, Elijah, to tell Ahab the rain was on its way. There was absolutely no sign of rain in the sky, but Elijah obeyed and told King Ahab to prepare for the rain to finally come. So Elijah said to Ahab, "You better get ready, because I hear the sound of an abundance of rain. You better prepare for a downpour."

Notice that the drought lasted three long years. In our lives, certain trials last much longer than others. We would like all of them to be short-lived, but that is not always the case. During those times of lengthy trials, we often become weary. We feel we need to see some sign from God, even a small one, that He is working on our situation and we will soon see a breakthrough.

What are we supposed to do during these times? For one thing, we should speak in faith. We should say what we need and want, not what we have. Like Elijah, we should say, "It's going to rain." In other words, whatever blessing we need God to send into our lives, we should speak as though it is already happening. We are not lying when we do this because, in the spiritual realm, our needs are being met. We are simply waiting for the manifestation of what God is already doing. If you are with someone who might not understand your declarations of faith, then simply say, "I believe God is taking care of this problem right now."

I do not believe Elijah actually heard the sound of rain in the physical realm. He heard it in the spiritual realm, by faith. He was listening to the Spirit of God; he believed what God said; he announced it to Ahab; and he began to act on it *before* he saw it manifest.

You, too, may be waiting on a word from God to come to pass. You may not see anything yet, but can you hear anything with your spiritual ears? By faith can you believe your blessing is on the way? The enemy may have your blessing dammed up, but the Holy Spirit is pressing against the dam right now, and it is about to burst.

Hold Your Position

And Elijah went up to the top of Carmel; and he bowed himself down upon the earth and put his face between his knees and said to his servant, Go up now, look toward the sea. And he went up and looked and said, There is nothing. Elijah said, Go again seven times.

1 Kings 18:42–43

After announcing to Ahab that rain was coming, Elijah went to the top of Mount Carmel and got down on his knees with his forehead to the ground. In that position of worship, Elijah sent his servant to run back and forth several times to see if the rain had started.

Can't you just envision the scene when Elijah bowed down while his servant went to check to see if the clouds were moving in? As the servant looked for signs of rain, he must have been thinking, *Elijah has missed it this time. There is nothing going on. How long are we going to continue this nonsense?*

Seven times Elijah's servant returned with a bad report, but Elijah never got out of his position of worship. Just imagine how he must have felt every time his servant came back to tell him the rain had not yet begun to fall. But each time, Elijah simply said, "Go again."

Elijah's servant may have been saying to him, "Elijah, you must have misunderstood what you thought God spoke to you because *nothing is happening*; there's not even a cloud out there."

But each time, despite repeated negative reports, Elijah just said, "Go again." He refused to give up! He stayed right where he was, worshipping God.

Many times, our problem is that although we get into the right position to start with, when our situations don't seem to change fast enough for us, we change positions. We start calling people, asking them what they did when they were in the same circumstances, or we start reasoning about how we can change things. We must remember that those who trust in the flesh will be disappointed, but those who trust in God will never be disappointed or ashamed (see Romans 10:11). We should take our place in worship and stand firm. Instead of changing positions, we should look and keep looking for signs that our blessing is on its way. In God's timing, we will see Him begin to move on our behalf.

Worship strengthens our faith. Doubt could have caused Elijah to give up, but he continued in faith because worship kept him strong. Romans 4:8–20 tells us that Abraham had absolutely no human reason to hope. Doubt and unbelief came against him, but did not defeat him. He grew stronger and stronger as he praised and worshipped God. The same outcome seemed to happen for everyone else in the Bible who chose to praise and worship God in the midst of their battles, so we can be sure it will happen for us too as we praise and worship Him.

Elijah Outlasted His Enemy

And at the seventh time the servant said, A cloud as small as a man's hand is arising out of the sea. And Elijah said, Go up, say to Ahab, Hitch your chariot and go down, lest the rain stop you. In a little while, the heavens were black with wind-swept clouds, and there was a great rain.

1 Kings 18:44–45

Finally, after looking seven times, the servant came back and reported, "Well, I do see one small cloud about the size of a man's hand." I believe this teaches us that if we look really hard, we can always find a cloud of hope in our situations, even if it is just a tiny one. No matter how things appear, I am sure we can find at least that much hope to hang on to.

The cloud Elijah's servant saw had to look tiny against the vast expanse of the sky, but it was enough to get Elijah excited. Perhaps we, too, should get excited about what we do see, even if it's very small, rather than being depressed or discouraged about what we do not see yet.

As soon as Elijah received the report from his servant, he was bold enough to tell the servant to go announce to Ahab that he'd better head for home because the rain was on its way. Sure enough, in a short time the skies were black, and it began to pour. Elijah then started running so fast that he beat Ahab and his chariot to Jezreel, about twenty miles away (1 Kings 18:46). Can you imagine the look on Ahab's face when Elijah went running past him, maybe waving and saying, "I told you! See you in Jezreel!"

When the Spirit of God came on Elijah, he was able to outrun and outlast his enemy, King Ahab. He endured a time of testing, when he had to believe what God said without seeing anything. After that time, he was still in his position. He had worshipped God all the way through the trial, and we can do the same.

Likewise, when the Holy Spirit enables you and me, we will be able to outrun and outlast our enemy, Satan. God's Spirit does come upon us as we worship, and He empowers us to outlast our enemy. This is part of God's battle plan.

CHAPTER 14

God Means Good

As for you, you thought evil against me, but God meant it for good, to bring about that many people should be kept alive, as they are this day.

Genesis 50:20

You may remember the Old Testament story of Joseph, who rose to be second in command of all Egypt under Pharaoh after his brothers sold him into slavery and told his father he had been killed. Years later, when God had raised Joseph to a high position of authority in Egypt, his brothers came to Egypt to buy grain during the famine Joseph predicted. Later, Joseph arranged for his father, Jacob, his brothers, and all their families to move to Egypt to live out the rest of the famine in peace and prosperity.

When Jacob died, Joseph's brothers were afraid Joseph would try to take revenge against them for selling him into slavery years ago. In Genesis 50:20, Joseph assures them of his forgiveness. In addition to forgiving them, he also demonstrates a positive attitude, saying basically, "You meant this to harm me, but God meant it for good, to save many people from starvation."

It is amazing how many times Satan will set a trap for us, meaning it for our harm and destruction. But when God gets involved in a situation, He takes what Satan meant for evil and turns it into something that works for our good instead. No human being can make things work that way, but God can. He can take any negative situation and, through His miracle-working power, use it to make us stronger and more dangerous to the enemy than we would have ever been without it.

My own situation bears this out. I was sexually, mentally, and emotionally abused for many years during my childhood. This was certainly a terrible thing to happen to a child and definitely a work of the enemy, but God has worked it out for good. My mess has become my message; my misery has become my ministry, and I am using the experience I gained from my pain to help multitudes of others who are hurting.

I encourage you not to waste your pain. God will use it if you give it to Him. He has given me beauty for ashes, just as He promised in Isaiah 61:3, but I had to let go of the ashes. I had to learn to have a good attitude, as Joseph did, and I had to learn to let go of the bitterness, resentment, and unforgiveness I held toward the people who hurt me.

If Satan has already hurt you, don't let the pain go on and on by being bitter. When we hate people, we are only hurting ourselves more and more. Often the people we are angry at are enjoying their lives and are not the least bit concerned about how we feel toward them. Remember, God is your Vindicator, and when the time comes, He will bring justice. In the end, the meek inherit the earth, and God's enemies perish (see Psalm 37).

Let's look at the story of Esther and her people as another example of how God brings good out of evil.

Satan's Plan for Evil

And when Haman saw that Mordecai did not bow down or do him reverence, he was very angry. But he scorned laying hands only on Mordecai. So since they had told him Mordecai's nationality, Haman sought to destroy all the Jews, the people of Mordecai, throughout the whole kingdom of Ahasuerus.

Esther 3:5–6

If you are familiar with this story, you remember that King Ahasuerus chose Esther, the cousin and adopted daughter of a Jewish man named Mordecai, to be queen of his kingdom. How did this happen? She was taken into the king's harem as a young maiden, and I feel sure this was not the plan she had in mind for her life. This situation probably frightened her and may have even seemed unsafe at the time. She was in the harem for a period of time, being prepared to go before the king. When that time came, God gave her favor with him, and he chose her as his queen. Little did she know that God was putting her in position to save her nation.

Often we have a plan in mind for our lives, but something happens to interrupt it. We resist the change and are not happy about it, but no matter what we do, this new thing seems to be God's will for us. We cannot imagine how it could work out for good, but God has a plan that is much better than ours.

Mordecai, the man who raised Esther, was an attendant in the king's court and had an enemy named Haman, the king's highest official. Because Mordecai refused to bow down to him, Haman became angry and hatched a plan to destroy not only Mordecai but all the Jews along with him—not realizing Queen Esther was herself a Jew and was Mordecai's cousin.

In the Bible, some characters are types and shadows, or examples of God's enemies;

and in this story, Haman represents the devil himself. Haman had a plan to destroy God's people, just as Satan has a plan to destroy us because we belong to God.

In Esther's situation, the Bible tells us she was afraid of the decree Haman had issued against the Jewish people. However, Mordecai told her she was called to the kingdom for this very time (see Esther 4:14). In other words, her high position was her destiny. Mordecai also told her that if she did not do what God was asking her to do, she would perish with everyone else. She agreed to do whatever needed to be done. At great risk to herself, she invited the king and Haman to an intimate dinner where she hoped to expose Haman's evil plan to the king.

Mordecai was a wonderful, godly man who had once saved the king from a plot against him by two of his eunuchs, a deed recorded in the Book of the Chronicles in the king's presence, but one for which Mordecai had never been rewarded (see Esther 2:21–23). Later we will see how God rewarded Mordecai for uncovering this evil plot.

Mordecai was a man called and empowered to bring deliverance to God's people, just as you and I are called and empowered by God to bring deliverance and help to others in our day.

As we have seen, Haman represents Satan. Just as Haman had a plan to destroy Mordecai and the Jews, so Satan has a plan to destroy us. In Esther 5:14, we read about Haman's plan to destroy Mordecai:

Then Zeresh his wife and all his friends said to him, Let a gallows be made, fifty cubits [seventy-five feet] high, and in the morning speak to the king, that Mordecai may be hanged on it; then you go in merrily with the king to the dinner. And the thing pleased Haman, and he caused the gallows to be made.

Esther 5:14

Remember that besides personally planning Mordecai's death, Haman had also already issued an order (with the king's permission) that was proclaimed throughout the kingdom: On a certain day all the Jews were to be slaughtered and their possessions taken from them. Esther 3:13 says, "And letters were sent by special messengers to all the king's provinces—to destroy, to slay, and to do away with all Jews, both young and old, little children and women, in one day...and to seize their belongings as spoil."

So Haman had laid a plan for the complete destruction of God's people, one that seemingly could not be changed because it had been issued under the authority of the king's name. But God had a different plan, and at just the right time, He put it into action.

God's Plan for Good

On that night the king could not sleep; and he ordered that the book of memorable deeds, the chronicles, be brought, and they were read before the king. And it was found written there how Mordecai had told of Bigthana and Teresh, two of the king's attendants who guarded the door, who had sought to lay hands on King Ahasuerus. And the king said, What honor or distinction has been given Mordecai for this? Then the king's servants who ministered to him said, Nothing has been done for him.

Esther 6:1–3

One night when he had trouble sleeping, the king had someone read the Book of the Chronicles to him and heard that Mordecai had previously uncovered a plot to harm the king. You and I need to remember that whenever we do something good, God records it. He will not forget it. The day will come when our good deeds will be brought out into the open.

Every time we have prayed for others or given to them, every time we have submitted to authority when we wanted to rebel against it, every time we have confessed God's Word when our emotions were screaming at us to say negative things—each act of obedience is recorded and will be rewarded. Every time we have taken our position of faith, worship, and maintaining a good attitude, every time we have offered to God the sacrifice of praise, God remembers. He does not forget the things we have done right with pure hearts and right attitudes (see Hebrews 6:10).

Mordecai had been doing some good deeds, but he had not been making a big deal about them. He had simply done them in secret, unto the Lord. The Bible teaches us not to let our right hands know what our left hands are doing (see Matthew 6:3). This means to do what we feel God is leading us to do—do it for His glory, then forget it and go on about our business. It means not patting ourselves on the back or telling others what we have done, but simply knowing our rewards will come from God when the time is right.

Two Plans Come into Conflict

The king said, Who is in the court? Now Haman had just come into the outer court of the king's palace to ask the king to hang Mordecai on the gallows he had prepared for him. And the king's servants said to him, Behold, Haman is standing in the court. And the king said, Let him come in. So Haman came in. And the king said to him, What shall be done to the man whom the king delights to honor? Now Haman said to himself, To whom would the king delight to do honor more than to me?

Esther 6:4–6

Now we see the scenario coming right down to the wire. We see how the devil, whom Haman represents, is working his plan. But we also see how God is working His plan.

Because Haman was so full of pride, he couldn't possibly imagine the king would want to honor anyone other than himself. So he thought, *I'm about to be blessed, so I need to come up with something really good.*

Haman suggested to the king that the one he desired to honor should be given apparel the king himself had worn, a horse the king had ridden, and a royal crown. He also recommended that one of the king's most noble princes lead the honored man through the city and proclaim, "Thus shall it be done to the man whom the king delights to honor" (Esther 6:9).

Now, watch what happens when Satan's plan and God's plan come into conflict: "Then the king said to Haman, Make haste and take the apparel and the horse, as you have said, and do so to Mordecai the Jew, who sits at the king's gate. Leave out nothing that you have spoken" (Esther 6:10).

What the king, who represents the Lord in this story, was telling Haman was, "Every blessing you planned for yourself you are now going to confer on Mordecai. You are going to watch while I bless him." When God decides to bless someone, no person on earth can stop Him.

Satan has some dirty tricks in mind for each of us. He has a plan for our total destruction, just as Haman did for Mordecai and the Jews. But God also has a plan for us, and His plan will not be thwarted.

God's Plan Prevails

Then Haman took the apparel and the horse and conducted Mordecai on horseback through the open square of the city, proclaiming before him, Thus shall it be done to the man whom the king delights to honor. Then Mordecai came again to the king's gate. But Haman hastened to his house, mourning and having his head covered.

Esther 6:11–12

But that is not the end of the story. Not only did the Lord turn the tables on Haman so that he had to give Mordecai the honor he planned for himself; He also turned back on Haman the evil plan he devised for Mordecai.

When Haman later went to the dinner Queen Esther gave for him and the king, she revealed his wicked plot to kill her and her people. As a result, the king had Haman hanged on the gallows he had built for

Mordecai. Esther had worshipped God with her obedience and willingness to stay in a situation that was unpleasant to her. She was willing to lay aside her plan and accept God's plan, even though she did not understand it for quite some time. Each act of obedience is a type of worship that God does not ignore.

Just as Jehoshaphat's enemies and Gideon's enemies ended up slaughtering themselves, Haman's plans backfired on him. He himself suffered what he tried to inflict on Mordecai and the Jews.

In the end, Mordecai got Haman's house, which the king gave to Esther and Esther gave to Mordecai (see Esther 8:1–2). The king also gave Esther authority to send a letter in his name throughout the kingdom to reverse the order to have the Jews killed and their possessions taken from them.

When we keep our eyes on God, stand firm in faith, continue to worship, and continue to believe and speak God's Word, we will see the enemy's plans for evil in our lives work out for our good.

When it was all over, the Jews were honored and blessed, Queen Esther enjoyed even more of the king's admiration and respect, and Mordecai had been elevated to the position of second-in-command, under the king himself.

Notice that I said "When it was all over." Whatever is going on in your life that may be hard for you right now will eventually be over. As the saying goes, "This, too, shall pass!" I encourage you to look past the pain to the joy of obtaining the victory and the prize.

I believe the encouragement in Esther and Mordecai's story and throughout this book is something many people need right now—maybe even you. No matter what you are going through or what storms you are facing in life, take your position. Don't give up. Stand still. Enter God's rest. See the salvation of the Lord. Quit worrying and trying to figure out everything that is happening around you. And above all, worship God. Remember, no matter what your battle is, it is not yours; the battle belongs to the Lord, and He has a plan to bring you victory.

CONCLUSION

I believe that as a result of reading this book, you will begin to handle the tests, trials, and battles of your life in totally different ways than you have handled them before because you now understand God's battle plan. Even when you are faced with temptations, you will be strengthened to resist them by worshipping God. In this book, I have shared some truths that will help you enjoy your life and your walk with God more than ever. Our calling as believers is to enjoy God and to find pleasure in fellowship with Him.

If we are worried or trying to figure out how to solve our problems on our own, we are not fellowshipping with God. I remember one morning years ago when I sat down in a chair where I prayed every day and began to worry about whatever circumstances were happening in my life. Suddenly, I sensed the still, small voice asking me, "Joyce, are you going to fellowship with your problems or are you going to fellowship with Me?" God was willing to handle my problems if I was willing to surrender them and spend my time with Him. I had to remember to worship, not to worry.

I believe you are going to make so much progress in your life as a result of the lessons you have learned in this book that you will be amazed. I fully expect your life to be easier from this point forward. I don't mean you will never experience trials and testings, but as you worship God, you will find what I call a "holy ease" to your life. Worshippers find everything easier. Burdens lift as we worship, and we are free to enjoy where we are on the way to where we are going.

Remember, God is for you. He has a battle plan sure to bring you breakthrough, before you even encounter the storms of life. He has already made a way for the breakthrough and victory you need. So worship Him until you see it come to pass!

JOYCE MEYER is one of the world's leading practical Bible teachers. Her daily broadcast, *Enjoying Everyday Life*, airs on hundreds of television networks and radio stations worldwide.

Joyce has written more than 100 inspirational books. Her bestsellers include *Power Thoughts; The Confident Woman; Look Great, Feel Great; Starting Your Day Right; Ending Your Day Right; The Everyday Life Bible; Approval Addiction; How to Hear From God; Beauty for Ashes;* and *Battlefield of the Mind.*

Joyce travels extensively, holding conferences throughout the year and speaking to thousands around the world.

JOYCE MEYER MINISTRIES ADDRESSES

Joyce Meyer Ministries—United States
P.O. Box 655
Fenton, MO 63026
USA
(636) 349-0303

Joyce Meyer Ministries—Canada
P.O. Box 7700
Vancouver, BC V6B 4E2
Canada
(800) 868-1002

Joyce Meyer Ministries—Australia
Locked Bag 77
Mansfield Delivery Centre
Queensland 4122
Australia
(07) 3349 1200

Joyce Meyer Ministries—England
P.O. Box 1549
Windsor SL4 1GT
United Kingdom
01753 831102

Joyce Meyer Ministries—South Africa
P.O. Box 5
Cape Town 8000
South Africa
(27) 21-701-1056

OTHER BOOKS BY JOYCE

Look Great, Feel Great

*The Love Revolution**

*Making Good Habits, Breaking Bad Habits**

Never Give Up!

The Penny

Perfect Love (previously published as *God Is Not Mad at You*)*

The Power of Simple Prayer

*Power Thoughts**

The Secret Power of Speaking God's Word

The Secret to True Happiness

Start Your New Life Today

*You Can Begin Again**

DEVOTIONALS

Battlefield of the Mind Devotional

The Confident Woman Devotional

*Ending Your Day Right**

Hearing from God Each Morning

Love Out Loud

New Day, New You

The Power of Being Thankful

Power Thoughts Devotional

*Starting Your Day Right**

Trusting God Day by Day

*Also available in Spanish.